DEBBIE BROWN'S
Fairy Tale Cakes

Debbie Brown's
Fairy Tale Cakes

HAMLYN

For my children, Lewis, Laura and Shaun

All photographs specially taken by Clive Streeter, except for the following, which were
provided by the Reed Consumer Books Picture Library:
Food in Focus: 7,
Hilary Moore: 19.

First published in Great Britain 1995
by Hamlyn an imprint of Reed Consumer Books Limited
Michelin House, 81 Fulham Road, London, SW3 6RB
and Auckland, Melbourne, Singapore and Toronto

ISBN 0 600 58437 2

Produced by Mandarin Offset
Printed and bound in Hong Kong

Editors: Sasha Judelson and Isobel Holland
Art Editor: Lisa Tai
Design: Town Group Consultancy
Production Controller: Melanie Frantz

Contents

Basic Cakes

These cake recipes are used throughout the book. To make it easier to follow, the ingredients are set out in chart form with cake sizes indicated by numbers.

MADEIRA CAKE

Madeira cake has a moist texture, yet is firm enough for novelty cakes which require a lot of cutting and shaping.

PREPARATION TIME: about 15 minutes
COOKING TIME: see chart
OVEN: 160°C, 325°F, Gas mark 3

1 Grease the bakeware, line the base and sides with greaseproof paper and grease again.

2 Cream the butter and sugar until light, fluffy and very pale.

3 Sift the flours together. Beat the eggs into the creamed mixture, one at a time, following each with a spoonful of flour.

4 Fold the remaining flour into the creamed mixture, followed by the grated lemon rind.

5 Turn into the prepared bakeware and level the top. Bake in a preheated oven for the time suggested in the chart or until well risen, firm to the touch and golden brown.

6 Cool in the bakeware for about 10 minutes, then turn out on to a wire rack and leave until cold. Do not peel off the lining paper, but wrap the cake in foil or store in an airtight container for at least 12 hours before cutting.

Right: Madeira cake

MADEIRA CAKE

★ LITTLE MISS MUFFET ★ PUSS IN BOOTS ★ RUMPLESTILTSKIN ★ LITTLE JACK HORNER ★

	1 LITRE (2.2 PINT) OVENPROOF BOWL	15 CM (6 INCH) ROUND	2 x 8 CM (3½ INCH) DIAMETER BOWLS	7 CM (3 INCH) DIAMETER MUG
SIZE	1	2	3	4
butter or margarine	150g (5oz)	175g (6oz)	50g (2oz)	40g (1½oz)
caster sugar	150g (5oz)	175g (6oz)	50g (2oz)	40g (1½oz)
self-raising flour	150g (5oz)	175g (6oz)	50g (2oz)	40g (1½oz)
plain flour	65g (2½oz)	75g (3oz)	25g (1oz)	25g (1oz)
eggs	2 (size 1)	3	1	1 (size 4)
grated lemon rind	½ lemon	1 lemon	¼ lemon	¼ lemon
cooking time	1 hour	1 hour	35 minutes	35 minutes

MADEIRA CAKE

★ THE ELVES AND THE SHOEMAKER ★ LITTLE BOY BLUE ★ HANSEL AND GRETEL ★
★ RAPUNZEL ★ THE THREE LITTLE PIGS ★

SIZE	25 CM (10 INCH) SQUARE 5	13 CM (5 INCH) ROUND 6	20 CM (8 INCH) ROUND 7	20 CM (8 INCH) SQUARE 8
butter or margarine	350g (12oz)	50g (2oz)	350g (12oz)	350g (12oz)
caster sugar	350g (12oz)	50g (2oz)	350g (12oz)	350g (12oz)
self-raising flour	350g (12oz)	50g (2oz)	350g (12oz)	350g (12oz)
plain flour	175g (6oz)	25g (1oz)	175g (6oz)	175g (6oz)
eggs	6	1	6	6
grated lemon rind	2 lemons	¼ lemon	2 lemons	2 lemons
cooking time	1 hour	35 minutes	1½ hours	1¼ hours

VICTORIA SPONGE CAKE

A classic, light Victoria sponge mixture, which tastes extra rich when made with butter.

PREPARATION TIME: about 30 minutes
COOKING TIME: see chart
OVEN: 175°C, 350°F, Gas mark 4

1 Grease the bakeware and either dust with flour or line the base with grease-proof paper and grease again.

2 Cream the butter and sugar until light, fluffy and very pale, then beat in the vanilla flavouring.

3 Beat in the eggs, one at a time, following each with a spoonful of the self-raising flour.

4 Sift the remaining flour and fold it very gently into the mixture alternately with the water.

5 Turn into the prepared bakeware and level the top. Bake in a preheated oven for the time suggested in the chart or until well risen and firm to the touch. Turn out on to a wire rack and leave to cool.

QUICK MIX CAKE

This is a very simple cake to prepare and bake. It is moist and light but with a firm enough texture to allow for the cutting and shaping required.

PREPARATION TIME: about 5 minutes
COOKING TIME: see chart
OVEN: 160°C, 325°F, Gas mark 3

1 Grease the bakeware and dust with a little flour.

2 Put the butter or margarine, sugar, eggs, sifted flour, baking powder and vanilla flavouring into a large-sized mixing bowl.

3 Mix the ingredients together with a wooden spoon or hand-held electric mixer, then beat vigorously for 1-2 minutes until the mixture is smooth and glossy.

4 Turn into the prepared bakeware and level the top. Bake in a preheated oven for the time suggested in the chart or until risen and firm to touch.

5 Cool in the bakeware for about 10 minutes, then turn out on to a wire rack. When cold, store in an airtight container or wrap in foil and leave for at least 12 hours before cutting.

Right: Quick mix cake

VICTORIA SPONGE CAKE

★ TWINKLE TWINKLE LITTLE STAR ★ LITTLE RED RIDING HOOD ★
★ GOLDILOCKS AND THE THREE BEARS ★ SNOW WHITE AND THE SEVEN DWARFS ★
★ TWO LITTLE DICKY BIRDS ★ JACK AND THE BEANSTALK ★

SIZE	20 CM (8 INCH) SQUARE 1	25 CM (10 INCH) SQUARE 2	20 CM (8 INCH) ROUND 3
butter or margarine	225g (8oz)	275g (10oz)	225g (8oz)
caster sugar	225g (8oz)	275g (10oz)	225g (8oz)
vanilla flavouring	4 drops	5 drops	4 drops
eggs (size 1 or 2)	4	5	4
self-raising flour	225g (8oz)	275g (10oz)	225g (8oz)
cold water	1 tablespoon	1 tablespoon	1 tablespoon
cooking time	40 minutes	40 minutes	1 hour

QUICK MIX CAKE

★ SNOW WHITE ★ TWO LITTLE DICKY BIRDS ★ THUMBELINA ★ THE UGLY DUCKLING ★
★ JACK AND THE BEANSTALK ★

	20 CM (8 INCH) SQUARE	2 LITRE (4 PINT) OVENPROOF BOWL	1 LITRE (2.2 PINT) OVENPROOF BOWL	25 CM (10 INCH) SQUARE
SIZE	1	2	3	4
butter or margarine	275g (10oz)	275g (10oz)	175g (6oz)	350g (12oz)
caster sugar	275g (10oz)	275g (10oz)	175g (6oz)	350g (12oz)
eggs (size 1 or 2)	5	5	3	6
self-raising flour	275g (10oz)	275g (10oz)	175g (6oz)	350g (12oz)
baking powder	2½ teaspoons	2½ teaspoons	1½ teaspoons	3 teaspoons
vanilla flavouring	10 drops	10 drops	6 drops	12 drops
cooking time	1¼ hours	1¼ hours	1¼ hours	50 minutes

PINK MARBLE CAKE

This cake with its marbled appearance is something different, but certainly the look isn't hard to achieve.

PREPARATION TIME: about 15 minutes
COOKING TIME: see chart
OVEN: 160°C, 325°F, Gas mark 3

1 Grease the bakeware, line the base and sides with greaseproof paper and grease again. To line a bowl, cut a circle of greaseproof paper and line the base only.

2 In a mixing bowl, cream the soft margarine and sugar until pale in colour.

3 Sift the flours together. Beat the eggs into the creamed mixture, one at a time, following each with a spoonful of flour.

4 Fold the remaining flour into the creamed mixture.

5 Put half the creamed mixture into another bowl. Fold the pink food colouring and the raspberry flavour concentrate into one mixture only.

6 Fold the two creamed mixtures together again, until only slightly mixed.

7 Turn into the prepared bakeware and level the top. Bake in a preheated oven for the time suggested in the chart or until well risen, firm to the touch and golden brown.

8 Cool in the bakeware for about 10 minutes, then turn out on to a wire rack and leave until cold. Wrap the cake in foil or store in an airtight container for at least 12 hours before cutting. You need not worry about which marble effect appearance you get when you cut the cake. Any kind of marble effect will look attractive and is sure to delight all. This cake is light enough to take any colour icing.

Right: Pink marble cake

$\mathcal{P}$INK MARBLE CAKE

★ CINDERELLA ★ RAPUNZEL ★ JACK AND JILL ★
★ HANSEL AND GRETEL ★

SIZE	1 LITRE (2.2 PINT) OVENPROOF BOWL 1	20 CM (8 INCH) SQUARE 2	25 CM (10 INCH) ROUND 3	20 CM (8 INCH) ROUND 4	25 CM (10 INCH) SQUARE 5
soft margarine	150g (5oz)	275g (10oz)	350g (12oz)	175g (6oz)	350g (12oz)
caster sugar	150g (5oz)	275g (10oz)	350g (12oz)	175g (6oz)	350g (12oz)
self-raising flour	150g (5oz)	275g (10oz)	350g (12oz)	175g (6oz)	350g (12oz)
plain flour	65g (2½oz)	150g (5oz)	175g (6oz)	75g (3oz)	175g (6oz)
eggs	2 (size 1)	5	6	3	6
pink liquid food colouring	¼ teaspoon	½ teaspoon	½ teaspoon	¼ teaspoon	½ teaspoon
raspberry flavour concentrate	5 drops	10 drops	12 drops	6 drops	12 drops
cooking time	1 hour	1 hour	1¼ hours	50 minutes	1 hour

RICH FRUIT CAKE

This fruit cake recipe was given to me by my mother who has honed it to perfection after many years of baking. It really does make a sumptuously, delicious, dark and moist cake. This cake is suitable for any kind of celebration. Its firm, moist texture is perfect for the cutting needed in novelty cakes. Although the cake is at its best 3 months after baking, eating it before or after this time doesn't matter. Keep wrapped until you are ready to eat it.

PREPARATION TIME: 30 minutes
COOKING TIME: see chart
OVEN: 140°C, 275°F, Gas mark 2

1 Grease the cake tin, line with a double layer of greaseproof paper and grease again.

2 Quarter, wash and thoroughly dry the glacé cherries and then place in a large clean bowl.

3 Add the sultanas, currants, raisins, mixed peel, ground almonds, chopped nuts, grated lemon rind and mixed spice. Mix well.

4 In another bowl, cream the butter and sugar until light, fluffy and pale.

5 Beat the eggs into the creamed mixture, one at a time, following each with a spoonful of the flour.

6 Add the black treacle.

7 Fold in the remaining flour and add the dried fruit mixture.

8 Turn the mixture into the prepared tin and level the top, then make a dip in the centre with the back of a spoon.

9 Tie a double layer of brown paper round the outside of the tin to protect the cake during cooking and place on a baking sheet lined with a double layer of brown paper.

10 Bake for the suggested cooking time and test by inserting a skewer into the centre. If it comes out clean the cake is done. If not, put it back into the oven for about 10 minutes more and then check again.

11 Leave the cake to cool in the tin. When cold, remove from the tin and wrap in greaseproof paper, then in foil. A final wrap of clingfilm will help keep the cake moist during storage.

12 To improve flavour and lengthen keeping time, spoon several tablespoons of brandy or other spirit over the top.

Variation: If you would like to make this cake a little lighter in colour, replace the black treacle with 1 tablespoon of golden syrup and replace the soft brown sugar with 225g (8oz) caster sugar.

RICH FRUIT CAKE

★ THE PRINCESS AND THE PEA ★

SIZE	20 CM (8 INCH) SQUARE
currants	275g (10oz)
sultanas	425g (15oz)
raisins	150g (5oz)
glacé cherries	150g (5oz)
cut mixed peel	50g (2oz)
mixed chopped nuts	75g (3oz)
ground almonds	50g (2oz)
grated lemon rind	1 lemon
plain flour	300g (11oz)
mixed spice	2 teaspoons
butter	275g (10oz)
soft brown sugar	275g (10oz)
eggs (size 2)	5
black treacle	1 tablespoon
cooking time	4½ hours

Right: Rich fruit cake

Icings and Fillings

The following recipes include all the icings and fillings you will need throughout the book. For instructions on how to colour icing, see page 21.

FONDANT ICING

Fondant icing (sugarpaste) can be bought from cake decorating suppliers, supermarkets and other outlets. Some brands are easier to use than others, so it is best to try a few to find the one you work with best. The ready-made icing is usually of high quality, but if you prefer to make your own, here is the recipe. As a general rule, this icing is rolled to a thickness of 3 mm ($\frac{1}{8}$ inch) before use.

MAKES 675g (1$\frac{1}{2}$lb)
1 egg white
2 tablespoons liquid glucose
675g (1$\frac{1}{2}$lb) icing sugar, sifted
a little white fat (optional)

1 Put the egg white and liquid glucose into a bowl and gradually add the icing sugar. Stir until the mixture thickens.

2 Turn out on to a surface dusted with icing sugar and knead until the paste is smooth and silky. If the paste becomes a little dry and cracked, try kneading in a little white fat.

MODELLING FONDANT

This is fondant icing with gum tragacanth added. It makes the icing firmer and easy to shape into figures, animals and small objects but, once unwrapped, you have to work extremely quickly as it starts to dry after only a few minutes.

Below: Coloured rolled out fondant icing; Colouring fondant icing; Royal Icing

Gum tragacanth is available in powder form from cake decorating suppliers and some chemists.

MAKES 450g (1lb)
2 teaspoons gum tragacanth
450g (1lb) fondant icing

1 Put the gum tragacanth on a clean surface and knead into the fondant. Wrap in a polythene bag and leave for about 8 hours before use to allow the gum to take effect.

ROYAL ICING

When I first started cake decorating I was terrified of piping with royal icing and avoided it as long as I could, but once I started, I realized just how simple it really is. It is difficult to make up smaller quantities than the recipe given, but it can be stored in an airtight container in a cool place, such as a refrigerator, for approximately 10 days. It must be stirred thoroughly before use to bind together all the ingredients once again. If you do not stir thoroughly before use your icing will be difficult to work with and will not give a smooth finish.

See page 23 to find out how to fold a paper piping bag.

MAKES ABOUT 225g (8oz)
1 egg white
1 teaspoon lemon juice
225-250g (8-9oz) icing sugar, sifted

1 Put the egg white and lemon juice into a bowl and beat in the icing sugar, a little at a time, until the icing is smooth, white, and forms soft peaks when the spoon is pulled out.

2 Cover the bowl with the icing in it with a damp cloth, and leave to stand for 5 minutes to disperse any air bubbles before use.

SIMPLE PASTILLAGE

MAKES ABOUT 350g (12oz)
1 egg white
350g (12oz) sifted icing sugar
2 teaspoons gum tragacanth

1 Put the egg white into a mixing bowl. Using 275g (10oz) of the sifted icing sugar, add to the egg white a little at a time, beating well to make a stiff consistency, royal icing. Level the top and sprinkle the gum tragacanth evenly over the surface. Leave to stand for 10 minutes.

2 Turn out on to a work surface and knead together, incorporating the remaining icing sugar.

3 Wrap in a polythene bag and store in an airtight container.

Above: Hair piped from Royal icing. Royal icing is useful for piping and styling hair and sticking modelled items together.

SUGAR GLUE

Sugar glue is an invaluable aid when fixing figures and small pieces to a cake.

15g ($\frac{1}{2}$oz) simple pastillage
2 teaspoons cool boiled water

1 Break up the pastillage icing in a bowl and pour the water on top. Leave to soak for at least 30 minutes, then mix thoroughly to a thick paste.

2 Sugar glue can be used as soon as it is made. It will keep in an airtight container in the refrigerator for up to 10 days.

MARZIPAN

Ready-made marzipan or almond paste is widely available from most major supermarkets, especially at Christmas, but if you make your own you can vary the colour. For a white marzipan, replace the egg with 2 egg whites; for a brighter yellow version, use 2 egg yolks. As marzipan does not freeze well, it is best to make up only the required quantity.

MAKES 450g (1lb)
125g (4oz) icing sugar, sifted
125g (4oz) caster sugar
225g (8oz) ground almonds
1 egg, lightly beaten
1 teaspoon lemon juice
few drops of almond essence

1 Put the sugars and almonds into a bowl. Add the egg, lemon juice and almond essence and mix together until it forms a stiff dough.

2 Turn out on to a surface dusted with icing sugar and knead until smooth. Wrap in a polythene bag and store for 2-3 days.

APRICOT GLAZE

This is best made shortly before you need it. It can be made up to a week ahead and stored in an airtight container in the refrigerator, but it will have to be boiled and cooled again before use.

MAKES 150ml (¼ pint)
150g (5oz) apricot jam
2-3 tablespoons water

1 Put the jam and water into a saucepan and heat gently, stirring occasionally, until the jam melts. Simmer gently for 1-2 minutes.

2 Rub through a sieve and allow to cool slightly before using.

Variations: Apricot jam is probably the most versatile jam to use for making a glaze, because it is a fairly neutral colour. You could just as easily use the same quantities of raspberry jam and water to make a raspberry glaze. This should only be used on cakes where the icing is dark as it can show through the pale colours.

LEMON CURD

Lemon curd is ideal to use instead of apricot glaze on the light fruit cake or any of the sponge cakes. You can use the bought variety if you don't have time to make your own, but this recipe below is easy to make and tastes delicious. Once made it can be stored for up to 1 month in a cool place or for up to 3 months in a refrigerator.

MAKES ABOUT 675g (1½lb)
225g (8oz) sugar cubes
3-4 large lemons
125g (4oz) unsalted butter
5 eggs, beaten

1 Rub the sugar cubes on the rind of the lemons until they are well-coloured and have absorbed the zest of the fruit.

2 Squeeze the juice from the lemons, there should be approximately 400ml (14fl oz), if not squeeze another lemon.

3 Heat the butter slowly in a heavy-based pan until it has melted, then add the sugar cubes and lemon juice and carry on heating gently until the sugar has dissolved. Do not allow to boil.

4 In a large bowl, stir 1 tablespoon of the hot mixture into the beaten eggs, repeat twice more. This helps to prevent eggs curdling.

5 Pour the mixture back into the pan and heat gently, stirring with a wooden spoon, until the mixture thickens and coats the back of a wooden spoon. Do not allow to boil.

6 Pour into hot sterilized jars and cover.

Variation: This recipe is easily adaptable for oranges to make a tasty alternative.

Left: Marzipan; apricot glaze

BUTTER CREAM

Butter cream is easy to work with and has many uses when making novelty cakes. When used to cover the surface of a cake it can dry out quite quickly, which may stop the fondant sticking. If this happens, simply rework the butter cream or apply a little more.

MAKES 350g (12oz)
125g (4oz) butter or soft margarine
225g (8oz) icing sugar, sifted
few drops of vanilla flavouring
1-2 tablespoons milk or water

1 Put the butter in a bowl and cream until very soft.

2 Gradually beat in the icing sugar, adding vanilla to taste, and just enough milk or water to give a firm but spreadable consistency. If not using straightaway, store in an airtight container in the refrigerator for up to 1 week. Allow to return to room temperature before using.

VARIATION: **Chocolate Butter Cream**
Dissolve 1-2 tablespoons sifted cocoa powder in a little hot water to give a thin paste. Allow to cool slightly before beating into the butter cream in place of the milk.

CONTINENTAL BUTTER CREAM

A deliciously rich, smooth butter cream for sandwiching cakes together.

MAKES ABOUT 275g (10oz)
75g (3oz) caster sugar
4 tablespoons water
2 egg yolks
175g (6oz) unsalted butter

1 Put the sugar and water into a small, heavy-based saucepan and heat gently until the sugar dissolves completely.

2 Put a sugar thermometer into the pan, bring up to the boil, and then boil steadily for 2-3 minutes, until the syrup

Above left: Continental butter cream; above right: butter cream

reaches 110°C, 225°F. If you do not have a sugar thermometer, try the thread test: dip the back of a teaspoon into the syrup and pull the syrup away with the back of another spoon. It should form a thin thread. If this does not happen, boil for another minute and test again.

3 Put the egg yolks into a large bowl and whisk well (a hand held electric mixer is best, but a balloon or rotary whisk will do). Whisking constantly, pour the syrup in a thin stream on to the yolks (not on to the mixer or bowl). Continue whisking until the mixture is thick and cool.

4 In another bowl, cream the butter until soft and light, then beat in the egg yolk mixture a little at a time, until smooth and spreadable.

Equipment and Techniques

The following information outlines equipment and techniques that are useful to both the beginner and practised cake maker.

There are hundreds of items you can buy to help with cake decorating, but if you are not an avid cake maker and decorator and only make cakes when the need arises, there are plenty of items from your kitchen cupboards that you can use instead of going out and breaking the bank!

For baking the cakes, different containers such as ovenproof bowls and mugs can be put to excellent use. For any circles that need to be cut, instead of using special plain circle cutters, as a guide to cut around you can use cups, mugs and egg-cups of the required size.

For decorating cakes, a sharp knife, a rolling pin and a few cocktail sticks are essential, but the rest you can improvise with items from your kitchen.

Cake boards

Cake boards come in a variety of shapes and sizes and are usually covered in silver foil, although gold and metallic red are obtainable. To make your cake look even better, I recommend you cover the board with fondant icing. Alternatively you can use colour co-ordinating paper, as long as it is greaseproof. Glue the paper to the cake board with a mixture of 2 teaspoons flour mixed to a paste with a few drops of water. Brush thinly on to the surface of the board using a pastry brush, cover with the paper, then leave to dry.

Greaseproof paper piping bags

These can be purchased ready cut to shape in small and large sizes, but a triangular shape cut from a sheet of greaseproof paper or baking parchment will fold just as well (see page 23).

Piping nozzles

I recommend that you use good quality piping nozzles, which, although more expensive, do last a lifetime. The basic writing nozzles in sizes 1–4 are used in this book for piping royal icing and indenting shapes using both ends.

Small rolling pin

This is useful for rolling out small pieces of fondant icing as a large rolling pin can be quite clumsy.

Turntable

For easy access to all sides of the cake you are working on, I recommend that

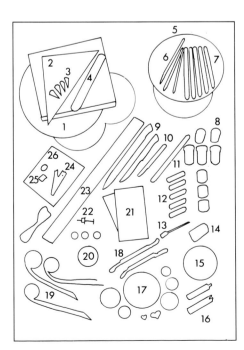

The following list is a guide to some of the useful items available from cake decorating suppliers (see page 87).

1 Cake boards
2 Greaseproof piping bags
3 Piping nozzles
4 Small rolling pin
5 Turntable
6 Paintbrushes
7 Food colouring pens
8 Food colouring pastes
9 Knives
10 Craft knife
11 Wooden and plastic skewers (dowelling)
12 Powder colours
13 Miniature brush
14 Gum arabic
15 Garrett frill cutter
16 Crimping tools
17 Basic cutters
18 Modelling tools
19 Ribbons
20 Pins
21 Smoother with handle
22 Plunger and blossom cutters
23 Ruler
24 Cocktail sticks
25 Embossing stamps
26 Foam

you use a turntable. The one shown here is metal, which can be quite expensive, but cheaper plastic ones are obtainable. If you prefer, an upturned tin could be used.

Paintbrushes

I recommend that you use good quality sable paintbrushes as they do not shed hairs like the cheaper versions. The basic sizes shown here should be enough to start.

Food colouring pens

These are felt tip pens filled with food colouring and come in a rainbow of colours and are extremely useful. Always use them after the icing has dried as the colour can spread.

Food colouring pastes

These come in a vast range of colours, but the basic primaries, red, blue, yellow and black are all you need to start with as you can mix these to achieve different colours.

Knives

To help with your cake decorating, make sure you have good sharp knives to work with in a variety of sizes.

Craft knife

Very useful for cutting out small pieces of fondant. Replacement blades can be purchased.

Plastic skewers (dowelling)

These are used to help support the cakes that stand quite high.

Powder colours

These come in a variety of colours, plain or lustre. Brushed on with a dry paintbrush, they give just a hint of colour or sparkle, but can be quite messy to use. You can also mix the powders to a paste with a few drops of clear alcohol or water and use for painting on to dry icing, which is especially effective with the silver and gold lustre powders.

Miniature brush

Very helpful in brushing away any loose icing sugar left on the cake and as it is so small, it will get to any awkward corner.

Gum arabic

Available from any cake decorating supplier, this white powder is used as a glue to stick items on to cakes. Mix together a small amount with a few drops of water.

Garrett frill cutter

This garrett frill cutter has a removable inner circle so you can use other circle cutters to change the depth of the frill (see page 22 on how to make a garrett frill).

Crimping tools

These are available in many shapes and are used to make patterns by gently pinching the fondant icing together. It is often used to create a decorative border on the fondant icing covered cake board.

Basic cutters

There are many special cutters which are available in different sizes and designs. A basic set of plastic or metal circle cutters are especially useful.

Modelling tools

These can work out to be expensive items. However, children's plastic craft tools available from toy and craft shops work out much cheaper and do the job just as well.

Ribbons

Using ribbons with co-ordinating colours and patterns for the cake board banding, adds the finishing flourish to your cake. Remember, if you are going to ice the board, you will need a slightly wider ribbon than if you do not. Use a pin to hold the ribbon in place at the back of the board. If you don't want the pin to show, you can disguise it with a small ribbon bow.

Pins

Pins are used to hold the ribbon banding in place on the cake board. They can also be used to make small marks or patterns on the icing.

Smoother with handle

This is used for smoothing out any dents in the icing to get a good finish. To use the smoother see page 22.

Plunger and blossom cutters

These blossom cutters attach to the end of the plunger and when used, make a prettily-shaped flower with an indented centre. When making the blossoms always push out on to a piece of foam as this helps to give shape to the flower and they also dry more quickly. Different shapes can be bought to attach to the plunger, such as a bow shape.

Ruler

Used for any accurate measuring required, but also for any straight line you wish to mark into the fondant icing.

Cocktail sticks

These are used to add colour to the icing (see page 21), and they have no end of uses when making modelled items or marking details on a cake.

Embossing stamps

These are designs with a raised outline, which when pushed gently into fondant icing, make an impression.

Foam

Your modelling work dries much quicker if placed on a piece of foam, as the air can circulate underneath as well as above. Foam is also used when making plunger flowers, as the centre of each flower is pressed into the foam to give it more shape.

Edible Glue

To store your edible glue conveniently use a small bottle with a brush attached to the lid. These are available from cake decorating suppliers (see page 87).

COLOURING METHODS

I recommend you use the paste or concentrated liquid food colouring obtainable from cake decorating suppliers. The liquid form sold in most supermarkets can make your icing too wet, especially if you have to achieve a deep colour. However, it is fine if only a pale shade is required.

Powdered food colouring can be quite messy, so it is best to use it only for dusting on when the icing is dry to achieve just a hint of colour. Edible gold and silver powder can be painted on to the icing after mixing with a few drops of clear alcohol, such as vodka or gin, or just plain water.

Food colouring pens come in many shades and avoid the need for paintbrushes. Only use the pens on icing that has had at least a day to dry out and before you start, brush off any excess icing sugar from the surface to prevent the food colouring from spreading out. If you have difficulty obtaining these pens, you can paint on the dry icing using concentrated food colouring that has been watered down to a watercolour paint consistency. Again, thoroughly brush off any loose icing sugar to prevent the colour from spreading.

How to colour fondant

Put a little colour on the end of a cocktail stick and add to the fondant. Fold it in and knead thoroughly until the colour is even throughout, with no streaks. If you require a deep colour, keep adding more food colouring a little at a time until you achieve the shade you want.

How to colour royal icing

Put a little colour on the end of a cocktail stick, add to the royal icing and stir well. You will find that this icing takes colour very easily and bright colours such as red and yellow can get brighter, so leave the royal icing covered with a damp cloth for a few minutes for the colours to develop.

How to roll out fondant

Take the required amount of fondant and knead it a little to warm it up. Dust the surface liberally with icing sugar to prevent the paste from sticking. Press the fondant on to the icing sugar, turn over and press again, then roll out the fondant, moving it around frequently

Above: Royal icing in a rainbow of pastel colours

so that it doesn't stick to the surface. Continue rolling out until it is about 3 mm (⅛ inch) thick.

Helpful Hints

The following tips are intended to give helpful advice and practical information to instructions that arise throughout this book.

How to smooth a cake surface

Cake smoothers are invaluable, as your hands alone will not get a perfect surface. They are relatively cheap and are available from cake decorating suppliers. The cake smoother with a handle is best for novelty cakes as it has rounded edges. Rub the surface of the cake in a circular motion, pressing quite firmly to remove any dents in the fondant.

Joins in the fondant should be removed before the icing starts to dry by rubbing with your fingers in a circular motion.

How to stick pieces of fondant together

A little water applied with a fine paint-brush will stick fondant icing together, but it is not strong enough for large pieces or for your modelling fondant figures. I recommend you use a little egg white or, if you prefer, gum arabic, which is an edible glue available in powder form from cake decorating suppliers. For an even stronger glue make sugar glue (see page 15).

How to make a garrett frill

Garrett frill cutters are available from cake decorating suppliers. Alternatively you can use a fluted cutter and a smaller plain cutter to achieve the same effect. Roll out a small amount of fondant quite thinly and cut with the garrett frill cutter or fluted and plain cutters. Using a cocktail stick dipped in cornflour, roll the end of the stick over each loop gently until the icing becomes thin and starts to frill. Work round until the circle is completely frilled, then cut open. Dampen the surface of the cake with a little water to stick the garrett frill in place.

How to mix colouring pastes and gold and silver lustre powders for painting

Clear alcohol should be used in preference to water, as it evaporates more quickly. For the colouring pastes, place a quantity of alcohol into a small bowl and using a cocktail stick dip it into the paste and add to the alcohol. Keep adding a little at a time until the desired colour is achieved. For the gold and silver lustre powders, mix 1 teaspoon of clear alcohol with $1/2$–1 teaspoon of powder to make a soft paste.

How to cover a cake board with fondant icing

Roll out the fondant icing. Dampen the cake board with a little water, then place the icing on the board and smooth with a cake smoother to get a completely flat surface. Trim the edges with a sharp knife.

How to grease and line a baking tin or ovenproof bowl

Place the cake tin on to a sheet of clean greaseproof paper and mark the outline with a pencil. Cut around the outline using a pair of sharp scissors. To measure the sides of the tin, take a piece of string and wrap it round the outside, use this to cut out another piece of greaseproof paper. Melt a little butter or margarine in a saucepan, then brush a thin coat on to the inside of the tin. Position both the cut-out base and sides inside the tin. Brush another thin layer of grease over the paper.

If you need to line an ovenproof bowl, cut a small circle out of grease-proof paper, large enough to cover the base only. Brush the inside of the bowl with melted fat, then position the cut-out paper in the bottom of the bowl.

How to make blossom flowers

The easiest way to make small blossom flowers is to use a blossom plunger cutter. The blossom cutters come in varying sizes and each attach to the end of a plunger. Push the end of the plunger cutter into the rolled out fondant icing to cut out a flower. Gently wipe the edges of the flower cutter with your thumb to remove any loose particles, then rest the plunger cutter on a piece of foam. Holding the plunger like an injection needle, push out the fondant flower into the foam to indent the centre. If you don't want to pipe a centre with royal icing, push the tip of a plain piping nozzle in the middle of the flower to mark the centre.

How to crimp using a crimping tool

Hold the crimping tool between your thumb and index finger, push the crimping tool into the icing, squeeze the two handles of the tool gently together and release very carefully, making sure it does not spring back. It is worth practising with some icing trimmings before you first use a crimping tool.

ℋOW TO MAKE A GREASEPROOF PAPER PIPING BAG

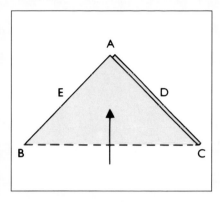

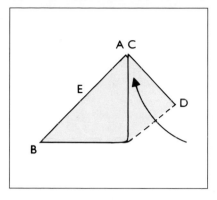

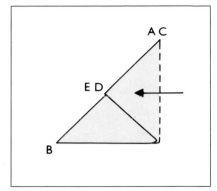

1 Cut a 25 cm (10 inch) square and fold to form a triangle.

2 Fold point C across to point A and crease firmly.

3 Fold point D and point E and again, crease firmly.

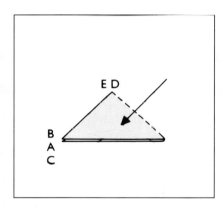

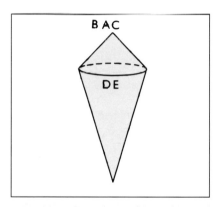

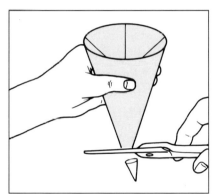

4 Fold point AC down to point B and crease firmly. Holding the bag at ED, open it out to make a cone.

5 Secure the join well with some adhesive tape and fold the top part down firmly inside the cone.

6 Cut off the tip of the paper bag so that the nozzle will fit neatly with about one-third of it showing.

ℱACTS AND FIGURES

• Unless otherwise stated, all spoon measurements given in this book are level and all eggs are size 2.

• Both metric and imperial measurements have been calculated separately. Use one set of measurements only as they are not exact equivalents. In some recipes, you may find an apparent discrepancy in the imperial equivalent. This is done to ensure a correct proportion of ingredients.

• Cooking times may vary slightly depending on the individual oven. Cakes should be placed in the centre of the oven unless otherwise specified. Always preheat the oven to the specified temperature.

• All icing is assumed to be coloured before you start following the recipe and all basic cakes baked. For detailed instructions on how to colour all kinds of icing see page 21.

• All icing used should be rolled to a thickness of 3 mm (⅛ inch) unless otherwise stated.

• All skewers in the text refer to plastic or wooden dowelling that can be bought from hardware stores and specialist cake decorating suppliers.

• Atmospheric conditions can affect drying times because icing absorbs moisture.

Rapunzel

Rapunzel! Rapunzel! Let down your hair
So I may climb your golden stair

You will need:
1 Madeira cake (size 5)
575g (1lb 4oz) fondant icing
green, mauve, brown, pink, flesh,
   yellow, black, blue and orange
   food colouring paste
575g (1lb 4oz) butter cream
egg white or gum arabic
1.445kg (3lb 4½oz) modelling
   fondant
25g (1oz) royal icing
black food colouring pen

Equipment:
25 cm (10 inch) oval cake board
cocktail sticks
8 cm (3 inch) and 11 cm
   (4 inch) plain circle cutters
foam sheet

fine paintbrush
large star piping nozzle
large and small blossom plunger
   cutters
piping bag

Colour:
Fondant icing: 425g (15oz) green,
   150g (5oz) dark green
Modelling fondant: 925g (2lb 1oz)
   dark mauve, 75g (3oz) mauve,
   150g (5oz) pale mauve, 75g (3oz)
   brown, 15g (½oz) pink, 15g
   (½oz) flesh, 50g (2oz) yellow, 5g
   (¼oz) black, 15g (½oz) white, 15g
   (½oz) blue, 5g (¼oz) pale orange,
   50g (2oz) dark green, 50g (2oz)
   light green
Royal icing: 25g (1oz) white

1 Using half of the green fondant, cover the cake board completely and then put aside to dry.

2 Slice the top off the cake so it is completely flat. The depth of the cake should measure 4 cm (1½ inches) and no deeper.

3 Using the 8 cm (3 inch) circle cutter, cut out 6 circles, then cut one circle using the 11 cm (4 inch) circle cutter. Put the cake trimmings aside for later.

4 With 225g (8oz) of the butter cream, sandwich 5 of the smaller circle cakes together. Place the remaining 8 cm (3 inch) circle cake on top of the

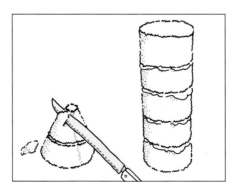

11 cm (4 inch) circle cake. Trim around the sides to make the sloping roof. Using 250g (9oz) of butter cream, sandwich the top layers together, then spread a thin layer of butter cream over the surface of the tower and roof to help the fondant stick.

5 Roll out 750g (1lb 11oz) of the dark mauve modelling fondant into an oblong measuring at least 25 x 30 cm (10 x 12 inches). Place the tower cake down on to it and roll the fondant around the tower. Trim at each end and at the join. Leave to dry on a sheet of foam for at least 8 hours, or overnight.

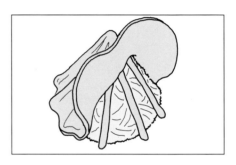

6 With the remaining dark mauve modelling fondant, roll 9 thin strips and stick evenly around the roof cake, trimming to fit, then roll out the remaining fondant and cover the roof completely. Mould around the strips with your hands, then cut a straight edge between each one at the base. Model the tiny teardrop shape for the top of the roof and stick in place with a little egg white. Reserve the trimmings.

7 When dry, place the tower upright on the centre of the cake board. Using the mauve and half of the pale mauve modelling fondant, model the stones in different sizes, pressing each quite flat. Using a little egg white, stick the stones on the tower one at a time in a haphazard pattern, letting some of the background show through. Leave a space uncovered at the front for the window, 2 cm (1 inch) from the top.

8 For extra support, cut some of the cake trimmings into different shapes and build them up against the base of the tower. Spread the remaining butter cream over the surface, reserving a little to stick the roof on later.

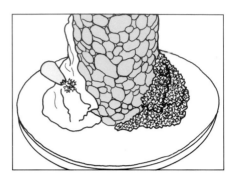

9 To make the bushes, knead the dark green fondant, the remaining green fondant and one third of the brown modelling fondant together until streaky. Thickly roll out and position around the bottom half of the tower, securing it with a little egg white. Press into the fondant over and over with the tip of the large star piping nozzle to give a rough leafy effect.

10 Roll out half of the remaining pale mauve modelling fondant. Place the roof cake down on to it and trim to fit, cutting inwards so the ridge is hidden. Stick the roof on top of the tower using the remaining butter cream. Thinly roll out the pale mauve modelling fondant trimmings and cut a strip for the window arch. Stick in place with a little egg white and trim to fit. Mark the stone pattern with a knife.

11 Thickly roll out the remaining pale mauve modelling fondant and cut out the windowsill and 5 blossom flowers using the large blossom cutter. Cut each flower exactly in half, then stick evenly under the roof for the supports and 1 under the windowsill, using a little egg white. Reserve the trimmings.

12 To make Rapunzel, model a bodice and 2 sleeves using half of the pink modelling fondant. Push the tip of a cocktail stick into the end of each sleeve to widen and make room for her hands. Stick in position at the window using a little egg white, marking the pleats on her shoulders with a cocktail stick.

13 Using the flesh modelling fondant, make two heads, four hands and two tiny noses. Stick the noses in place and position one head at the window for Rapunzel. Mark a smile on both faces using a cocktail stick.

14 To make Rapunzel's hair, thinly roll out the yellow modelling fondant and cut thin strips, 2.5 cm (1 inch) in length, 20-25 strips at a time. Twist these strands together, sealing each end with a little egg white. Make nine of these and stick in place winding down the tower. Cut more strips and build up her hair on top of her head a little at a time. Tease the strands in place using a damp paintbrush. Cover each join in the hair rope with 2-3 tiny strands for the banding. Stick Rapunzel's hands in place holding her hair.

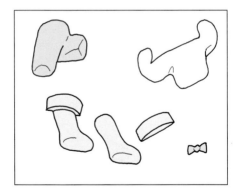

15 To make the prince, cut the black modelling fondant in half and model two boots with strips wrapped around the top for the flaps. Model the trousers and a tiny hairband using a 5g (¹/₄oz) piece of the dark mauve modelling fondant trimmings. Roll a ball with half of the white modelling fondant, flatten slightly then make two cuts either side. Use to model the prince's top and stick in place with the trousers and boots in his pose against the tower. Stick his head and hands in position.

16 Roll out the blue modelling fondant and cut a triangular shape for the cloak measuring no more than 5 cm (2 inches) in length. Using a little egg white to stick, wrap round the prince, pleating at the top using a cocktail stick. With the pale orange modelling fondant, cut thin strips for the hair as before and stick to his head, teasing in place with a damp paintbrush. Stick the hairband in place.

17 Using the blue modelling fondant trimmings, model a small bird and mark the feathers. With the remaining white modelling fondant, model two more birds. Cut 6 tiny triangular shapes for the three beaks and two white patches for the blue bird. Stick everything together and put aside to dry.

18 To make the thornbush, roll out three-quarters of the remaining brown modelling fondant into a long thin sausage shape, stick to the bushes in a twisted pattern. Leave to set for 10 minutes. Take the dark green and light green modelling fondant and the remaining brown modelling fondant and knead until streaky. Model 3 more long thin sausage shapes and entwine each around the brown vine, building up the thornbush a little at a time.

19 Knead the mauve, blue, pink and yellow modelling fondant trimmings together until streaky. Roll out and cut the flowers using the small blossom plunger cutter.

20 Place the royal icing into a piping bag and snip the end so you have a small hole. Pipe the thorns by touching the tip of the piping bag on the thornbush, squeeze gently and pull up sharply. Stick all the flowers and birds in place. Leave everything to dry for at least 8 hours, or overnight.

21 With the black food colouring pen draw the eyes on Rapunzel, the prince and the three birds.

Jack and The Beanstalk

*"Fee, fi, fo, fum,
I smell the blood of an Englishman"*

You will need:

1 Quick mix cake (size 4)
  or 1 Victoria sponge cake (size 2)
4 tablespoons lemon curd
1.200kg (2lb 10oz) fondant icing
blue, green, brown, red, flesh,
  yellow and plum food colouring
  paste
650g (1lb 8oz) modelling fondant
egg white or gum arabic
black food colouring pen

Equipment:

25 cm (10 inch) square cake board
25 x 30 cm (10 x 12 inch) oblong
  cake card
strong non-toxic tape or 6 flat-
  headed pins
cocktail sticks
large star piping nozzle
fine and medium paintbrushes
small pieces of foam
large blossom cutter

Colour:

Fondant icing: 350g (12 oz) pale
  blue, 150g (5oz) light brown, 700g
  (1lb 9oz) green
Modelling fondant: 225g (8oz) green,
  250g (9oz) white, 75g (3oz) light
  brown, 25g (1oz) blue, 50g (2oz)
  red, 5g (¹/₄oz) flesh, 15g (¹/₂oz)
  yellow, 5g (¹/₄oz) plum

1 Tape or pin the cake card securely to the back of the cake board.

2 Using the pale blue fondant, cover the cake card completely for the sky. Position the cake on to the cake board.

3 Cut a 10 cm (4 inch) strip from the front of the cake tapering in to only 2 cm (1 inch) for the pathway. Trim the top of the cake from the right-hand corner so it slants downwards to the opposite corner. Trim the edges off the cake to round off. Build up the right-hand side of the cake for the grass using some of the cake trimmings and sandwich the trimmings in place with a little of the lemon curd. Using a knife spread a thin layer of the remaining lemon curd over the surface of the cake to help the fondant stick.

4 Thickly roll out the light brown fondant and cover the front of the cake board for the pathway. Mark the uneven surface, with a paintbrush. With some of the light brown fondant trimmings, model all the stones and the mushroom stalks. Push some of the smaller stones on to the path.

5 Roll out the green fondant and cover the cake completely, trimming the edge in line with the cake board. Using the tip of the star piping nozzle, press into the fondant over and over to make the grass. Stick all the stones and mushroom stalks in place.

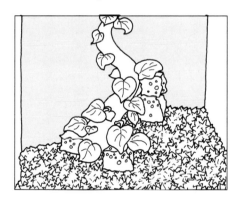

6 To make the beanstalk, roll out 150g (5oz) of the green modelling fondant into a long sausage shape thinner at one end. Stick in place, curling up the cake card. With the remaining green modelling fondant, model the curly stalks, all the leaves for the beanstalk and the flowers on the grass, all in different sizes, marking the centre vein with a knife. Reserve one small leaf and curly stalk, stick the remaining pieces in place, using a little egg white or gum arabic. Use small pieces of foam for support whilst drying.

7 Make the three clouds using the white modelling fondant and stick to the top of the cake card, using a little egg white or gum arabic. Pinch with your fingers to shape. Stick the curly stalk and leaf on to the centre cloud, using a little egg white or gum arabic.

8 Using 50g (2oz) of the light brown modelling fondant, make the giant's boot, with a strip modelled for the boot flap. Mark the creases with a cocktail stick and position up against the cloud, sticking with a little egg white or gum arabic.

9 To make Jack, model his trousers first using a 15g (½oz) piece of the blue modelling fondant and stick in position against the beanstalk. With the remaining blue modelling fondant, make his hat and two circles for each sleeve.

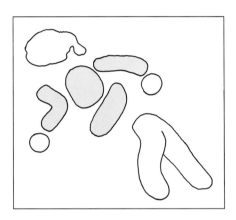

10 Make Jack's top, using a 25g (1oz) piece of the red modelling fondant. First roll a ball, flatten slightly and cut two arms either side. Smooth to remove the edges then stick in position on the beanstalk. Model the base of his jacket and wrap around the top of his trousers. Stick the two blue sleeve ends in place.

11 Roll a ball for his head, a tiny nose and make Jack's two hands, using the flesh modelling fondant. Stick in place and mark his smile with a cocktail stick. Position his hat on his head.

12 Reserve a 5g (¼oz) piece of the light brown modelling fondant, then with the remaining piece make Jack's boots and treasure sack and stick in place.

13 Using 15g (½oz) of the red modelling fondant, model eight mushrooms and stick each in place on the stalks.

Stick little flattened balls on to each mushroom to represent the spots, made from the remaining light brown modelling fondant.

14 Mix some water with a little of the brown food colouring paste. Using the medium paintbrush, paint a thin layer over the pathway, stones and the giant's boot.

15 Using the yellow modelling fondant and the large blossom cutter, make 18-20 flowers and position on the grass.

16 Make all the tiny balls for the beanstalk and each flower centre, using the remaining red modelling fondant trimmings and then stick these tiny balls in place.

17 Using the plum modelling fondant, model five beans and then scatter them all around the bottom of the beanstalk.

18 Colour a little of the brown modelling fondant trimmings dark brown and stick on to Jack's head for his hair. Use a cocktail stick to curl. Leave the cake to dry for at least 8 hours, or overnight.

19 Using the black food colouring pen, draw the birds on the cake card and draw in Jack's eyes.

Right: Jack and the Beanstalk

Alternative design:

Instead of the sack Jack is carrying you could model the goose with its golden eggs. Using 5g (¼oz) of white modelling fondant make the goose marking the feathers, beak and feet with a cocktail stick. Use another 5g (¼oz) of white modelling fondant and make 3 or more eggs. Apply edible gold leaf to make the golden colour. If you want to make it easier dust the eggs with gold lustre powder.

Snow White and the Seven Dwarfs

"Mirror, Mirror on the wall,
Who is the fairest of us all?"

You will need:

1 Quick Mix cake (size 1) or
  Victoria Sponge (size 1)
1.600kg (3lb 9oz) fondant icing
brown, bright blue, yellow, red,
  black, green and flesh food
  colouring paste
375g (13oz) butter cream
sugar glue
250g (9oz) simple pastillage
blue, red, green, mauve, orange,
  yellow, pink, brown and black
  food colouring pens
1.100kg (2lb 7oz) modelling fondant
edible gold leaf
100g (4oz) royal icing

Equipment:

30 cm (12 inch) square cake board
ruler
cocktail sticks
fine & medium paintbrushes
4 cm (1½ inches) circle cutter
no. 3 piping nozzle

Colour:

Fondant icing: 350g (12oz) light
  brown, 750g (1lb 11oz) white,
  500g (1lb 2oz) blue
Modelling fondant: 150g (5oz)
  yellow, 375g (13oz) red, 275g
  (10oz) green, 150g (5oz) flesh,
  75g (3oz) black, 50g (2oz) light
  brown, 25g (1oz) white
Pastillage: 250g (9oz) blue
Royal icing: 50g (2oz) black, 50g
  (2oz) white

1 Cover the cake board with the light brown fondant icing. Mark the lines 2.5 cm (1 inch) apart with a ruler. Using a cocktail stick, mark the woodgrain pattern. Water down a little of the brown food colouring paste with one tablespoon of water. Using the medium paintbrush, paint a thin coat over the surface of the floorboards to highlight the woodgrain. Then put aside to dry.

2 Cut the cake as shown below.

3 Cut a layer in the bed cake and sandwich back together using half of the butter cream. With the remaining butter cream, spread a thin layer over the surface of all the cakes to help the fondant stick.

4 Thinly roll out 300g (11oz) of the white fondant and with it cover the bed completely. Model a pillow using 125g (4oz) of the white fondant icing, position the pillow on the bed and press down on the centre to make a dip as if a head had rested on it.

5 Reserve 75g (3oz) of the white fondant, then thickly roll out the remaining white fondant and cut an oblong measuring 25 x 15 cm (10 x 6 inch). Shape each corner and rub the edges to soften and round off. Place over the bed for the cover. Mark the deep creases of the blanket with your fingers. The creases should be quite obvious. Then position the bed on the cake board.

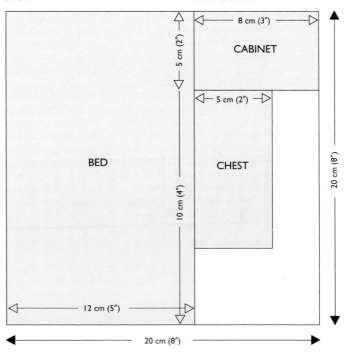

6 Using half of the blue fondant icing, roll out and put the base of the cabinet cake down on to it and trim to fit. Cover the back, then the two sides in the same way. Cover the front and mark the doors with a knife. Cut a piece slightly larger for the top, soften the edges to round off and position on the top of the cabinet. Using a cocktail stick, mark the woodgrain pattern. Model 6 balls, 4 large and 2 small. Stick the 4 large balls to the underside of the cabinet using a little sugar glue and stick the 2 smaller balls on to the doors.

7 To cover the chest, roll out the remaining blue fondant icing. With the blue fondant icing cover the back first, followed by the two sides, then the top, rounding off the edges as before. Mark the woodgrain pattern with a cocktail stick and put aside to allow it to dry.

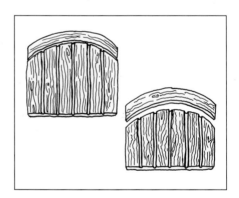

8 Using the blue pastillage, make the headboard and the footboard. Cut a square for the headboard measuring 11 cm (4¹/₂ inches). Trim an arch in the top and mark the wooden slates with a ruler. Mark the woodgrain with a cocktail stick as you make each item as this icing dries quickly. Cut a strip and stick on the top of the headboard following the arch. Do the same for the footboard which is 2.5 cm (1 inch) less in height.

9 Thickly roll out the remaining blue pastillage and cut out 4 posts, 1 cm (¹/₂ inch) in width, 2 measuring 12 cm

Above: A close-up showing the intricate detail of the painted patchwork quilt.

(4¹/₂ inches) in height for the headboard and the other 2 measuring 10 cm (4 inches) for the footboard. With the trimmings, roll 4 balls for the top of the posts. Leave to dry out on a completely flat surface.

10 Dilute a little of the bright blue food colouring paste with 1 tablespoon of water. Using a medium paintbrush, paint a thin coat over the cabinet, chest, headboard and footboard to highlight the woodgrain pattern. Leave everything to dry for at least 8 hours, or overnight.

11 Using the food colouring pens, draw the patchwork quilt. Mark the stitching with the black pen.

12 For the sheet, roll out the remaining white fondant into an oblong measuring 25 x 5 cm (10 x 2 inches). Mark the sheet edge with a knife. Place the sheet on the bed, tucking under the top of the patchwork quilt.

13 Using the sugar glue, stick both the headboard and the footboard in place.

Put the cabinet in position and put the chest at the foot of the bed, it should be pressed gently against the footboard.

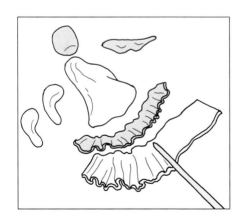

14 To make Snow White, take half of the yellow modelling fondant and model her skirt, marking the pleats with a knife. With the remaining yellow modelling fondant, model the tiny candle flame and put aside for later, then model the 2 sleeves, wider at one end for the puff, marking the pleats with a cocktail stick. Roll out and cut an oblong 23 cm (9 inches) in length for the frill. Roll the end of the paintbrush along one side of the frill to gather it up slightly.

15 With a 50g (2oz) piece of the red modelling fondant, model Snow White's bodice, the waist frill and make the skirt frill as before but smaller in depth.

16 With the black modelling fondant, model the candle holder and cut a strip for Snow White's bodice. Make 14 little boots and cut 14 thin strips for the top of the boots. Put the strips under a polythene bag to stop them drying out before use.

17 Assemble Snow White in her pose on the bed, sticking the pieces in place with a little sugar glue. Put the yellow frill in place first at the foot of the bed with the red frill arranged on top. Place the skirt on next. Put the bodice in position with the waist frill and wrap the black bodice around her waist tucking in at the back. Put the arms in position.

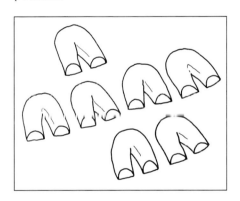

18 Divide 150g (5oz) of the green modelling fondant into 7 equal pieces and with it model the dwarfs' trousers. Put the trousers aside to dry for the moment, to be assembled later.

19 With the flesh modelling fondant, make 8 heads each weighing 15g (¹/₂oz). Also model 16 little hands and 8 tiny noses. Mark Snow White's mouth with a cocktail stick, 4 of the dwarfs' mouths with the tip of the No. 3 piping nozzle and the remaining dwarfs' mouths with the end of the paintbrush. Position Snow White's head, nose and hands in place, sticking with a little sugar glue.

20 Make each dwarf one at a time each in a different pose, using the sugar glue to stick the dwarfs in position. Stick the trousers to the boots with a black strip helping to hold the trousers in place and then stick on the cake board. Each top is made with a 35g (1¹/₂oz) piece of the red modelling fondant with the bottom hollowed out slightly to fit over the top of the trousers.

21 Cut a circle for each collar using the 4 cm (1¹/₂ inch) circle cutter and position on the top, then stick the head, nose and hands in place. Model each hat using a 25g (1oz) piece of modelling fondant. Make four of the dwarfs with green hats and the remaining 3 with red hats.

22 Using the light brown modelling fondant, model 7 little treasure sacks, 5 unopened, 1 with the top open and the last one over the dwarf's shoulder with a small split cut in the base. Put a small piece of the light brown modelling fondant underneath the split for the gold treasure and fill the open sack with light brown modelling fondant.

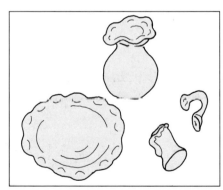

23 Model the candle, jug and bowl with the white modelling fondant. Pinch around the edge of the bowl and top of the jug with your fingers. Model the handle, marking the details with a cocktail stick. Position the jug and bowl on the chest, sticking together with the sugar glue. Put the candle on to the candle holder with the yellow flame on top, then place on the cabinet.

24 Using the edible gold leaf, cover the light brown modelling fondant in the open sack and the spill on the floor. Mark two gold crosses on Snow White's bodice.

25 With the white royal icing and the No. 3 piping nozzle, pipe the dwarfs' hair, eyebrows and long pointed beards.

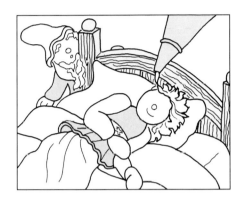

26 With the black royal icing and the No. 3 piping nozzle, pipe Snow White's hair, letting it fall on to the pillow. Leave everything to dry for at least 8 hours, or overnight.

27 Using the black food colouring pen, draw all the eyes, Snow White's eyebrows, the dotty pattern on the water jug at the foot of the bed and all the patches on the dwarfs' clothes.

Alternative design:

To simplify this cake you could make a larger bed without the cabinet and chest and have the quilt one colour. To cut down on the modelling, you could make all the dwarfs in bed with their little faces peeping over the top of the sheet.

The Elves and the Shoemaker

*The elves set to work with their little fingers, stitching
and hammering, swiftly and lightly*

You will need:

1 Madeira cake (size 8)
1.6kg (3lb 7oz) fondant icing
brown, mauve, green, flesh, cream
  and yellow food colouring paste
275g (10oz) butter cream
3 tablespoons lemon curd
egg white or gum arabic
425g (1lb 1oz) modelling fondant
brilliant silver lustre powder
50g (2oz) royal icing
black and peach food colouring
  pens

Equipment:

32 cm (13 inch) octagonal cake
  board

ruler
cocktail sticks
fine and medium paintbrushes
no. 3 piping nozzle
medium calyx cutter
foam pieces
greaseproof paper piping bags

Colour:

Fondant icing: 675g (1lb 6oz) light
  brown, 925g (2lb 1oz) mauve
Modelling fondant: 75g (3oz) mauve,
  75g (3oz) green, 75g (3oz) flesh,
  75g (3oz) light brown, 50g (2oz)
  dark brown, 75g (3oz) white
Royal icing: 25g (1oz) cream, 25g (1oz)
  dark brown

1 Cover the cake board with 375g (13oz) of the light brown fondant icing. Using a ruler, mark the two lines for the wooden planks and mark the wood-grain pattern with a cocktail stick. Water down a little of the brown food colouring paste with one tablespoon of water. Using a medium paintbrush, paint a thin coat over the surface of the cake board to highlight the woodgrain pattern and put aside to dry.

2 Slice the top off the cake so it is completely flat. Cut a 2.5 cm (1 inch) strip from one side of the cake, then cut the cake exactly in half lengthways.

3 Cut a dip in the top of each cake 1.5 cm ($^1/_2$ inch) deep. Start cutting 2.5 cm (1 inch) from one end and stop 5 cm (2 inch) from the opposite end.

4 Cut a 5 cm (2 inch) dip centrally on each side to shape the shoes.

5 Trim off the four corners of each shoe to round off, then trim all around each cake to remove the edges.

6 Trim around the base of each shoe at an angle so the fondant can easily be tucked around. Cut a slight dip just above the heels at the back to shape.

7 To give a little more height, slice a layer in each shoe and sandwich back together using all of the butter cream.

8 Spread a thin layer of lemon curd over the surface of each cake to help the fondant icing stick.

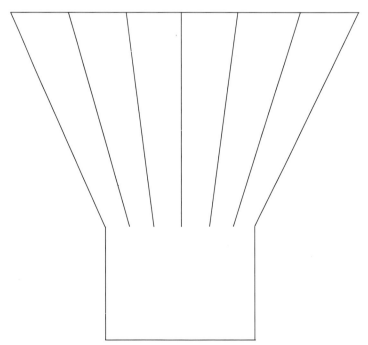

Shoe flap template

9 Roll a long sausage shape using 50g (2oz) of the mauve fondant and cut in half. To give each shoe more height, place the sausage shapes around the shoe openings and smooth in line with the surface of the cake. Using 75g (3oz) of the mauve fondant, cut in half and 'pad' out each toe area.

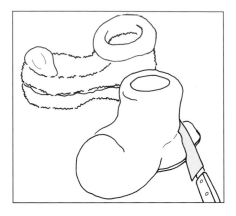

10 Using 400g (14oz) of the mauve fondant icing for each shoe, roll out and cover the two cakes completely. Smooth in around the base and trim.

11 To make the shoe soles, roll out the remaining light brown fondant icing and put the shoes down on to it, one at a time, and cut around. Mark the heel lines with a knife. Position each shoe on the cake board, sticking in place with a little egg white or gum arabic. Press the tip of the piping nozzle into the heel of the shoe on its side to mark the tacks, and mark the stitching around the edge with a cocktail stick.

12 Using the template and the mauve modelling fondant, cut out two shoe flaps. Make five cuts in each and mark the stitching with a cocktail stick. Using a little egg white or gum arabic, overlap each cut, stick in place on the shoes.

13 To make the two elves, cut a 50g (2oz) piece of the green modelling fondant in half. Roll sausage shapes with each and cut to make the two legs. With the remaining green modelling fondant and the medium calyx cutter, roll out and cut the two collars and cut

the two hats with the modelling fondant thicker in the centre. Pinch the top of each hat to shape. Put the trimmings aside for later.

14 To make the elves' bodies, roll two 25g (1oz) balls using the flesh modelling fondant and flatten each slightly. Make two cuts either side and model the arms. With the remaining flesh modelling fondant, make the two heads, four feet and two tiny noses.

15 Assemble the elves on the cake in their poses, sticking them in place with a little egg white or gum arabic. Use pieces of foam for support whilst drying, if necessary. Mark the smiles with a cocktail stick.

16 Model the glue pot with the light brown modelling fondant and put aside to dry.

17 With the dark brown modelling fondant make the glue pot stick, two twigs for the thread, the spike base and the tiny hammer handle. Mark the woodgrain pattern on each with a cocktail stick. Push the end of a paintbrush into the top of the spike base to make a hole for the spike to sit in. With some of the mauve and green modelling fondant trimmings, wrap around the twigs, sticking them in place, and mark the thread lines with a knife.

18 Using 50g (2oz) of the white modelling fondant, make the candle and candle holder. Roll out the remaining white modelling fondant and cut the two buckles and model the hammer

head, the spike, four needles and all the tacks. Knead a tiny amount of yellow food colouring paste into some trimmings, model the candle flame.

19 Mix some of the brilliant silver lustre powder with two teaspoons of water to make a paste. Using a medium paintbrush, paint a thin coat over the candle holder, the buckles, the hammer head, the needles, the spike and all the tacks. Paint a little on the shoe heel to highlight the tacks, using a fine paintbrush. Leave to dry for 10 minutes, then paint on another thin coat. Leave everything to dry for at least 8 hours, or overnight.

20 When everything is completely dry, assemble the pieces on the cake and board, sticking them in place with a little egg white or gum arabic. With the light brown and mauve modelling fondant trimmings, roll very long thin sausage shapes for the needle and reel thread and stick in place.

21 Using the cream royal icing and a greaseproof paper piping bag, pipe the glue in the glue pot.

22 Pipe the hair, using the brown royal icing and piping nozzle. To make it spikey, pull the nozzle away sharply.

23 With the peach food colouring pen, colour in the centre of the flame on the candle. Using the black food colouring pen, draw the elves' eyes and colour in the shoe openings to give depth.

Puss-in-Boots

Puss wanted the giant's castle for his master
So he asked "Can you change into a tiny mouse?"

You will need:

5 Madeira cakes (size 1, size 2, size 3 and size 6)
1.650kg (3lb 11oz) fondant icing
red, black, pink and green food colouring paste
575g (1lb 4oz) butter cream
580g (1lb 4¼oz) modelling fondant
50g (2oz) royal icing
egg white or gum arabic
brilliant silver lustre powder
black food colouring pen

Equipment:

25 cm (10 inch) round cake board
cocktail sticks
fine and medium paintbrushes
10 cm (4 inch) plain circle cutter
plastic skewer or dowelling
no. 2 plain piping nozzle

Colour:

Fondant icing: 750g (1lb 11oz) red, 600g (1lb 5oz) black, 300g (11oz) white
Modelling fondant: 225g (8oz) white, 350g (12oz) black, 5g (¼oz) pink
Royal icing: 50g (2oz) white

1 Cover the cake board with 250g (9oz) of the red fondant icing and put aside to dry.

2 Slice the top off all the cakes so that they are completely flat. Slice a layer in the centre of the larger round cake and sandwich the smaller round cake in between. Position the bowl cake on top of the round cakes.

3 To mark the arms, make a cut about 1 cm (½ inch) deep near the top of the bowl cake, and continue to cut in a curving line down to the bottom of the bowl cake. Mark the back of the arm curving similarly 5 cm (2 inches) behind the first line. Repeat for the other arm.

4 Slice downwards at the back, keeping the bottom area rounded, and trim round to the arms. Slice down the front, keeping the tummy area just a little rounded, again trim round to the arms.

5 Slice out a piece of cake directly underneath each arm and in between to separate. Trim the base of the cake to make the feet and trim out a thin wedge at the front and back to mark the legs. Trim the edges off the arms and trim any angles that are left round the cake.

6 Sandwich the three layers of the cake together with half of the butter cream and place the cake in the centre of the cake board. Spread a thin layer of butter cream all over the cake to help the fondant icing stick.

7 Sandwich the two small bowl cakes together with butter cream for the head, trim the front slightly flat for the face. Spread a thin layer of butter cream all over the head and set aside.

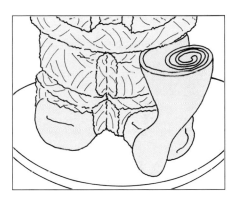

8 To give extra length to each boot, split a 75g (3oz) piece of the black fondant icing exactly in half and 'pad' out each toe. Roll out 400g (14oz) of the black fondant icing into an oblong measuring at least 45 cm (18 inches) in length and cut a straight line along the top. Roll up the fondant icing, then unroll around the bottom half of the cake, keeping the straight edge for the top of the boots. Rub the join closed at the back with your fingers and trim around the base.

9 Using the black fondant icing trimmings, cut two thin strips for the sole of each boot and stick in place around the base of the cake. Roll out the remaining black fondant icing and cut into two strips, each measuring 20 cm (8 inches) in length and 2.5 cm (1 inch) in width for the boot flaps. Stick in place around the top of each boot and smooth the edges to round off.

10 To make the jacket, roll out the remaining red fondant icing and then cut an oblong measuring 12 x 45 cm (5 x 18 inches). Roll up the fondant icing lengthways, then carefully unroll it around the top part of the cake, keeping the join at the front for the jacket opening. Smooth around the arms and upwards to the shoulders with your hands and trim to neaten. Mark the arm creases with the end of a paintbrush.

11 To make the collar, thickly roll out 125g (4oz) of the white fondant icing and cut out a circle using the circle cutter. Push the end of a paintbrush in around the edge to frill and position the collar on top of the cake.

12 Split a 50g (2oz) piece of the white fondant icing exactly in half and one piece in half again. Use the largest piece to 'pad' out the nose area on the small round cake and the two remaining pieces to pad out the cheeks. Roll out 125g (4oz) of the white fondant icing and cover the face completely, tucking the fondant icing around the head. Rub the join closed with your fingers. Position the head on the body and push the skewer or dowelling down through the top to keep it in place.

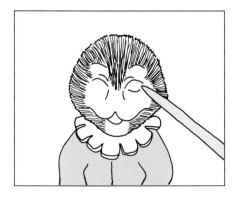

13 Mark all the fur with a knife. Make a cut for the mouth and pull slightly downwards to open. Mark Puss's smile and press your finger into each corner to indent. Mark his eyes and eyebrows. Using a cocktail stick, mark the whiskers either side of his nose.

14 Model the two paws using 50g (2oz) of the white modelling fondant for each. Mark the claws with a cocktail stick then, using a little egg white or gum arabic, stick in position. Roll a long sausage shape with another 50g (2oz) piece and stick to the back of the cake for Puss's tail. Model the two ears with a 25g (1oz) piece of the white modelling fondant split exactly in half. Mark all the fur with a knife.

15 Mix a little of the black food colouring paste with two teaspoons of water. Paint a thin coat over Puss's head, paws, ears and tail, using the medium paintbrush. Keep the brush quite dry so a little white fondant still shows through.

16 With 25g (1oz) of the white modelling fondant, roll out and cut two cuffs and two shoe buckles. With some of the black fondant trimmings, model the two buttons for the cuffs. Stick everything in place with a little egg white or gum arabic.

17 Roll a ball with 75g (3oz) of the black modelling fondant and model a dome shape for the top of the hat. Position on top of Puss's head. Trim out a piece at either side and slot in the two ears. Roll out another 75g (3oz) and cut out a strip for the hat rim measuring 30 cm (12 inches) in length. Cut the top edge with a slight point in the centre. Wrap around his ears and the top of the hat, sticking in place with a little egg white or gum arabic.

18 To make the feather, roll a sausage shape thinner at one end using a 50g (2oz) piece of the white modelling fondant. Flatten slightly and indent down the centre and mark the feathers with a knife. Arrange on the hat following the hat rim and stick in place.

19 Roll out the remaining black modelling fondant and from it cut out the cloak, which should measure 18 cm (7 inches) in width at the top, 30 cm (12 inches) at the base and 15 cm (6 inches) in length. Roll over the top to make a collar and wrap around the back of the cake, sticking in place with a little egg white or gum arabic.

20 To make the mouse, split a 25g (1oz) piece of the white modelling fondant into two pieces. Roll a ball for the body with the first piece and model the head with the other. With the white modelling fondant trimmings, make two arms, two ears and a tail and assemble everything together in Puss's paws. Mark the mouse's mouth with the end of a paintbrush and the smile and whiskers with a cocktail stick.

21 Using the pink modelling fondant, make the nose and inner ears for the mouse and the nose and mouth for Puss. Knead a tiny amount of the green food colouring paste into some of the white modelling fondant trimmings and make Puss's eyes. Model the pupils with a tiny amount of the black modelling fondant trimmings. Stick everything in place with a little egg white or gum arabic.

22 With the white royal icing and the piping nozzle, pipe the tiny dots on Puss's eyes to give a sparkle, pipe all the dots around the base of his jacket and the cake board. Leave the cake to dry for at least 8 hours, or overnight.

23 Mix a little of the silver lustre powder with 2 teaspoons of water to make a paste. Paint a thin coat over the edging on the jacket, the edge of the cake board and over the shoe buckles. Leave to dry for at least 10 minutes, then paint another thin coat.

24 Outline Puss's eyes and draw his eyelashes with the black food colouring pen.

Right: Puss-in-Boots

Hansel and Gretel

*The house of candy was built
to tempt children in*

YOU WILL NEED:

1 Pink marble or Madeira cake
  (size 5)
950g (2lb 1oz) fondant icing
green, pink, brown, mauve, yellow,
  blue, flesh, peach, black and cream
  food colouring paste
500g (1lb 2oz) butter cream
1.325g (2lb 15oz) modelling fondant
egg white or gum arabic
50g (2oz) royal icing
2 tablespoons granulated sugar
black food colouring pen

EQUIPMENT:

25 cm (10 inch) petal-shaped
  cake board
cocktail sticks
fine and medium paintbrushes
medium heart cutter
2 cm (³/₄ inch), 3 cm (1 inch) and
  miniature circle cutters
no. 3 plain piping nozzle
small star nozzle

COLOUR:

Fondant icing: 350g (12oz) green, 325g
  (11oz) white, 275g (10oz) pink
Modelling fondant: 675g (1lb 8oz) light
  brown, 75g (3oz) pale pink, 125g
  (4oz) pale mauve, 125g (4oz) dark
  pink, 25g (1oz) white, 25g (1oz)
  yellow, 125g (4oz) green, 25g (1oz)
  blue, 50g (2oz) flesh, 25g (1oz)
  peach, 50g (2oz) black
Royal icing: 25g (1oz) white, 25g (1oz)
  cream

1 Cover the cake board with 350g
(12oz) of the green fondant and put
aside to dry.

2 Slice the top off the cake where it has
risen so it is completely flat.

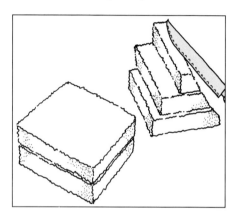

3 Cut the cake as shown below. Put
two 12 cm (5 inch) square cakes one
on top of the other and put aside. To
make the roof, put the three remaining cakes centrally one on top of the
other in order of size. Trim at opposite
sides, cutting downwards at an outward angle to make the sloping roof.
Stop cutting at the centre of the bottom
layer.

4 Using three-quarters of the butter
cream, sandwich all the cakes together and position the cake on the cake
board. Using the remaining butter
cream, spread a thin layer over the
surface of the cake to help the fondant stick.

5 Model the roof window, using a 50g
(2oz) piece of the white fondant and
position on the front of the cake.

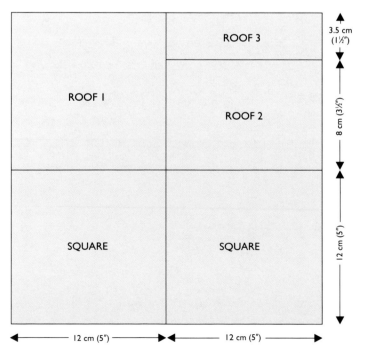

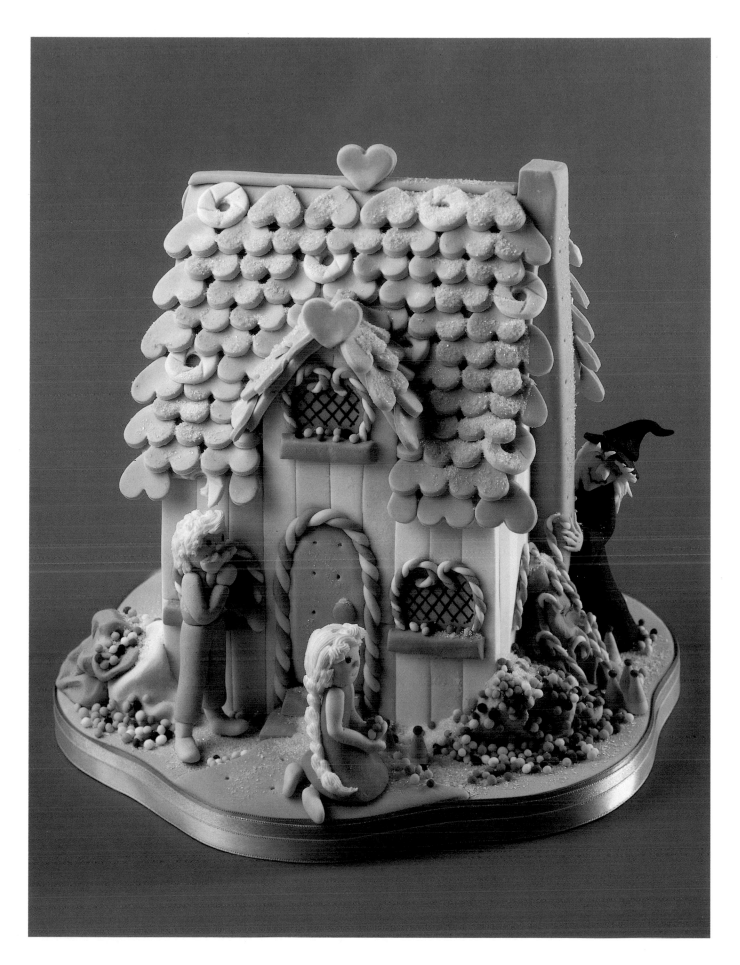

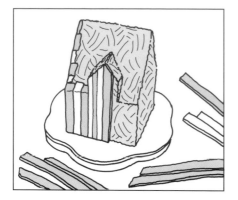

6 Using the pink fondant and the remaining white fondant, roll out and cut strips 1.5 cm (½ inch) in width. Stick on to the cake alternately, leaving the roof uncovered. Cut off each strip just above the bottom of the roof and smooth the edge in line with the surface of the cake.

7 Cut out spaces for the three windows, using the 3 cm (1½ inch) circle cutter, and cut a space for the door measuring 9 cm (3½ inches) in height.

8 To make the shortbread chimney, roll a long sausage shape at least 20 cm (8 inches) in height with 75g (3oz) of the light brown modelling fondant. Flatten the front and cut the sides, top and bottom straight. Mark the holes with a cocktail stick. Stick to the side of the house, using a little egg white or gum arabic.

9 Cut a 50g (2oz) piece of the light brown modelling fondant exactly in half. Model the door with one piece and press the other on to the board for the path. Leave enough room for the step. Mark the holes with a cocktail stick.

10 To make a base for the roof tiles, roll out 200g (7oz) of the light brown modelling fondant and cut two oblong shapes measuring 15 x 12 cm (6 x 5 inches). Cover each side of the roof, trimming around the roof window. Using the light brown modelling fondant trimmings, cover the top of the roof window, letting it overlap slightly.

11 Using 25g (1oz) of the pale pink modelling fondant and the 2 cm (¾ inch) circle cutter, roll out and cut sixteen circles. Cut a hole in each, using the miniature circle cutter and mark the pattern with a knife.

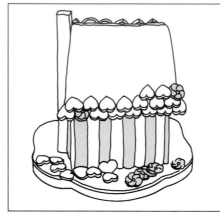

12 To make the tiles for the roof, roll out and cut heart shapes from the remaining light brown modelling fondant using the medium heart cutter. Position each tile on the roof, building up from the base and adding in the pink circle biscuits. With the trimmings, roll a long thin sausage shape and flatten slightly. Stick to the top of the roof and along the top of the roof window. Trim to fit and mark the holes with a cocktail stick. Make three more hearts and stick two of these back to back with an opening at the bottom. Stick this to the top of the roof and the remaining heart on the top of the roof window.

13 Using 25g (1oz) of the pale mauve modelling fondant and the 3 cm (1½ inch) circle cutter, cut out three circles and position one circle in each window.

14 To make the windowsills and the step, thickly roll out 25g (1oz) of the dark pink modelling fondant and cut 3 thin strips measuring 4 cm (1½ inches) in length and stick one each under a window. Cut out the two steps and stick them in place. Model a door handle with the modelling fondant trimmings and stick in place.

15 To make the candy window frames, roll 5g (¼oz) each of the dark pink and white modelling fondant into thin sausage shapes and twist together. Cut into six pieces 4 cm (1½ inches) in length and stick two at each window. Using 15g (½oz) more of each colour, make 8-10 candy canes and put aside to dry.

16 To make the door frame, twist together 5g (¼oz) each of the dark pink and yellow modelling fondant and position around the door, sticking with a little egg white or gum arabic.

17 Make the bushes using 50g (2oz) modelling fondant for each. Make two green, one dark pink, one pink and one pale mauve, and stick to the board with a little egg white or gum arabic. Pinch with your fingers to shape.

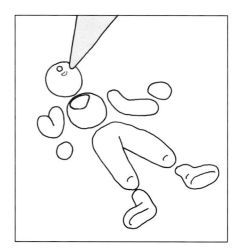

18 To make Hansel, roll a sausage shape with 15g (½oz) of the blue modelling fondant, make a cut for the two legs and model his trousers. Make his top using a 5g (¼oz) piece of the pale mauve modelling fondant and another 5g (¼oz) piece for his two arms. Cut a small triangle for Hansel's chest and stick in place with a little egg white or gum arabic. With a 15g (½oz) piece of the flesh modelling fondant, make his two feet, two hands, roll a ball for his head and make a tiny nose. Mark his open mouth with the tip of the No. 3 piping nozzle.

19 To make Gretel, model her dress using a 25g (1oz) piece of the peach modelling fondant and cut the bottom straight. Make her two feet, two arms, roll a ball for her head and make a tiny nose using 15g (½oz) of the flesh modelling fondant. Mark her smile with the tip of the No. 3 piping nozzle.

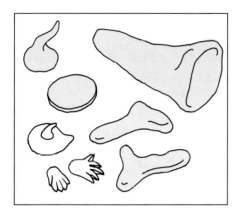

20 Model the witch's gown using a 25g (1oz) piece of the black modelling fondant. With the remaining black modelling fondant, make her two sleeves, model a circle for her hat rim and make the pointed hat. Model the witch's head, crooked nose and hands using the remaining flesh modelling fondant. Assemble all the figures together on the cake board, in their poses. Break off a piece of the pink roof biscuit and stick in Hansel's hand.

21 Make six rainbow cakes. Knead some of the dark pink and black trimmings together to get a plum colour. Model tiny rainbow drops using all the coloured modelling fondant trimmings and sprinkle over the bushes, sticking with a little egg white or gum arabic. Stick the candy canes on to the pink bush.

22 Slightly dampen the roof and bushes by brushing a little water over the surface using the medium paintbrush. Sprinkle on the granulated sugar.

23 Using the white royal icing and the No. 3 piping nozzle, pipe the witch's spikey hair.

24 Pipe Hansel's and Gretel's hair, using the cream royal icing and a small star nozzle. Leave the cake to dry for at least 8 hours, or overnight.

25 With the black food colouring pen, draw all the eyes and the witch's crooked smile. Draw the leaded window panes.

Alternative design:

To make this cake easier, you could replace the modelling fondant rainbow drop sweets with shop-bought sweets. Lollipops would make a good alternative for the trees, use other small sweets for the rainbow drops around the house. If you can find unusually shaped and coloured sweets they are bound to amuse and entice all those who eat this cake.

Thumbelina

*Thumbelina was scarcely half a thumb's length in height.
A neat polished walnut shell served as her cradle*

You will need:

1 Quick mix cake (size 2)
825g (1lb 13oz) fondant icing
peach, dark green, brown, flesh and
  egg yellow food colouring paste
250g (9oz) butter cream
275g (10oz) modelling fondant
egg white or gum arabic
50g (2oz) royal icing
yellow, peach, dark green and
  brown dusting powder

Equipment:

25 cm (10 inch) round cake board
fine and medium paintbrushes
cocktail sticks
10 cm (4 inch) plain circle cutter
greaseproof paper piping bag
large blossom plunger cutter

Colour:

Fondant icing: 250g (9oz) dark peach,
  450g (1lb) pale brown, 125g (4oz)
  white
Modelling fondant: 175g (6oz) dark
  green, 25g (1oz) flesh, 25g (1oz)
  pale peach, 25g (1oz) dark peach,
  25g (1oz) peach
Royal icing: 50g (2oz) dark yellow
  (egg yellow with a touch of
  brown)

1 Cover the cake board with the dark peach fondant. Roll out 50g (2oz) of the dark green modelling fondant and from it cut out a leaf measuring 18 cm (7 inches) in length. Using a knife, make small cuts around the edge then 'frill' the edge by rolling the paste quite thin. Mark the vein lines of the leaf with the back of a knife. Position the leaf on to the cake board and put it aside to allow it to dry.

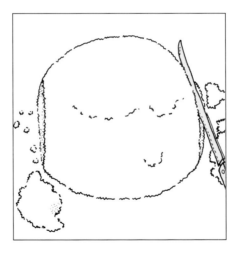

2 Slice the top off the cake so it is completely flat and turn over. Trim a little cake from opposite sides to make a slight oval shape.

3 Using three-quarters of the butter cream, spread a thin layer over the surface of the cake to help the fondant stick.

4 Thickly roll out the pale brown fondant and cover the cake completely. Trim around the base, leaving a 2 cm (1 inch) rim. Turn the cake over and smooth the rim in line with the top of the cake. Trim away any excess fondant to neaten. Using your fingers, pinch all round the top edge.

5 Mark the walnut shell pattern using the end of a paintbrush. Press the paintbrush in quite deep, then smooth out the groove with your fingers. Position the cake on the cake board.

6 Spread the remaining butter cream over the top of the cake. Roll out the remaining dark green modelling fondant into a circle to fit the top of the walnut shell. Smooth out the edge of the fondant to round off and then position on top of the cake.

7 Model the pillow using 75g (3oz) of the white fondant and then position the pillow on the bed. Roll a ball for Thumbelina's body, using the remaining white fondant, flatten out the ball slightly to give it a better shape and then position it on the bed so that it is placed just under the pillow.

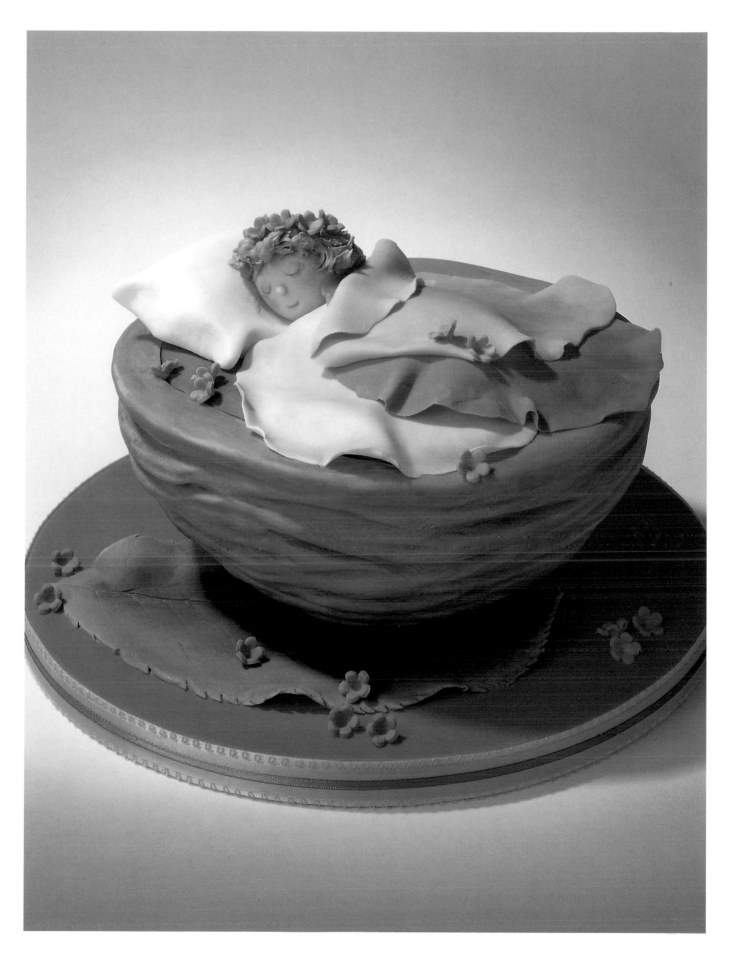

8 Roll a ball for Thumbelina's head and a tiny ball for her nose using the flesh modelling fondant. Stick in place on the pillow. Mark her eyes and mouth with a cocktail stick.

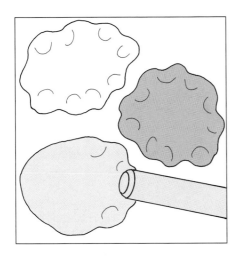

9 Make the three petal blankets using the pale peach, dark peach and peach modelling fondant and the 10cm (4 inch) plain circle cutter. Thin and frill around the edge of each petal blanket, using a rolling pin, and place the blankets over Thumbelina.

10 Pipe Thumbelina's hair using the dark yellow royal icing and the grease-proof paper piping bag with a small hole cut at the tip. 'Curl' the hair with a cocktail stick.

11 Knead the pale peach, peach and dark peach modelling fondant trimmings together until streaky. Using the blossom plunger cutter, make all the flowers. Stick a row of flowers on Thumbelina's hair for her crown and then scatter the remaining flowers around the cake and cake board.

12 Leave the cake to dry for at least 8 hours, or overnight.

13 Dust the petals and pillow with the yellow and peach dusting powder, using the medium paintbrush.

14 Dust the leaf with the dark green and brown dusting powders, using the medium paintbrush. Keep the dark green nearer the centre of the leaf and the brown just tinting the edge.

15 Rub a little peach dusting powder on to Thumbelina's cheeks to give her a blush.

16 Water down a little of the brown food colouring paste with one table-spoon of water. Paint Thumbelina's eyebrows and eyelashes using the fine paintbrush. With the remaining watered-down brown food colouring paste, paint a thin coat over the surface of the walnut shell using the medium paintbrush.

Alternative design:

To make this cake even prettier, you could rest the walnut shell on a lily pad. Make a large lily pad to fit the cake board using 275g (9oz) of green modelling fondant. You could make pastillage lily petals and position them around the bed to represent the inner petals of the lily. Place more petals around the base to finish the flower after leaving them to dry thoroughly, slightly curved in shape.

The Princess and The Pea

*Something small and hard found its way into the bed
For I am black and blue all over*

You will need:

1 Rich fruit cake (size 1)

1.6kg (3lb 9oz) fondant icing pink, brown, yellow, blue, mauve, flesh, green and cream food colouring paste

egg white or gum arabic

2¹/₂ tablespoons apricot glaze

1kg (2lb) marzipan

1 tablespoon clear alcohol

710g (1lb 10¹/₂oz) modelling fondant

75g (3oz) royal icing

blue and black food colouring pens

pink dusting powder

edible gold leaf

Equipment:

30 cm (12 inch) petal-shaped cake board

cocktail sticks

crimping tool

fine paintbrush

25 cm (10 inch) square cake card

3 m 45 cm (11¹/₂ ft) fine gold beading, 1 m 95 cm (5¹/₂ ft) large gold beading

pastry brush

ruler

no. 2 & no. 3 plain piping nozzles

rose embossing stamp

4 x 20 cm (8 inch) plastic dowelling or skewers

2 m 30 cm (7 ft 8 inches) of 15 mm dusky pink ribbon (including cake board banding)

clear tape

swag mould (optional)

foam sheet

straight garret frill cutter

small heart cutter

small pieces of foam

Colour:

Fondant icing: 500g (1lb 2oz) dusky pink (pink with a touch of brown), 1.100kg (2lb 7oz) white

Modelling fondant: 165g (6¹/₂oz) dark dusky pink, 430g (16oz) light dusky pink, 100g (3¹/₂oz) white, 15g (¹/₂oz) flesh

Royal icing: 50g (2oz) dusky pink, 25g (1oz) cream

1 Roll out 250g (9oz) of the dusky pink fondant icing and cover the cake board completely. Crimp a line all round the edge. Following the crimped line, stick the fine gold beading in place, using a little egg white or gum arabic.

2 Cut an oblong from the cake card measuring 25 x 14 cm (10 x 5¹/₂ inches). Roll out 175g (6oz) of the dusky pink fondant and cover completely, then put aside to dry.

3 Cut the cake exactly in half and put one on top of the other. Position the cake on the cake board.

4 Brush a little apricot glaze between the layers of the cake to stick them together, then brush the remaining apricot glaze over the surface of the cake, using the pastry brush, this will help the marzipan stick. Roll out the marzipan, measure and cut pieces to fit the sides and the top of the cake.

Cover the sides with marzipan first, then the top. Put the cake aside to dry for 24 hours.

5 Brush the surface of the marzipan with clear alcohol. Measure one end of the bed. Using 300g (11oz) of the white fondant, thickly roll out and cut two pieces to fit the bed at either end. Cover the two sides of the bed in the same way using 600g (1lb 5oz) of the white fondant.

6 Using a ruler or similar straight edge, mark the lines for the mattresses with narrower lines at the top for the quilts. Start from the base of the bed and work upwards. Mark the various patterns on the mattresses using a knife, the tips of the piping nozzles and a cocktail stick for different effects.

7 Measure the top of the bed. Roll out 150g (5oz) of the white fondant and cut a piece to fit. Smooth the edges to round off and position on top of the bed for the sheet. Model a pillow using the remaining white fondant, and stick in place with just a little egg white or gum arabic.

8 To make the bed cover, roll out 125g (4oz) of the dusky pink fondant, cut an oblong 18 x 15 cm (7 x 6 inches), then trim at each corner to round off. Cut a frill around the sides and the bottom using a knife. Position the cover on top of the bed, then stick a line of fine gold beading around the edge, following the frill.

9 Using 75g (3oz) of the dark dusky pink modelling fondant, cut a strip for around the base of the bed, 1.5 cm (½ inch) in depth. Stick in place using a little egg white or gum arabic. Gently press the rose embossing stamp into the strip to indent the pattern. Moisten the top of the strip with a little egg white or gum arabic, then stick the line of large gold beading in place.

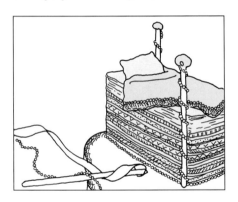

10 Wind the ribbon and fine gold beading around each dowelling and secure with clear tape. Split a 25g (1oz) piece of the light dusky pink modelling fondant into eight equal pieces. Push one on to each end of the dowelling, securing with egg white or gum arabic, stick one at each corner of the bed. Stick the covered cake card on top.

11 Using 300g (11oz) of the light dusky pink modelling fondant, make four sets of curtains. For this book, these were made using a mould for swags, but they can be modelled using a cocktail stick to mark the pleats. Make each curtain in two separate pieces, each piece measuring 10 cm (4 inches) in length. Leave to dry on a sheet of foam until the modelling fondant becomes

firm, then using the dusky pink royal icing and the No. 3 piping nozzle, stick each curtain in place. Position the lower curtains first so they help support the upper curtains whilst drying.

12 Using 15g (½oz) each of the light and dark dusky pink modelling fondant, roll thin sausage shapes and twist them together for the curtain tie-backs. With another 15g (½oz) of the light dusky pink modelling fondant, model four bows and stick in place with the tie-backs around each curtain to hide the join.

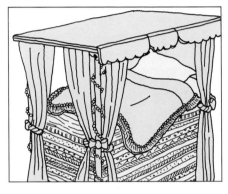

13 Roll out 75g (3oz) of the light dusky pink modelling fondant and using the straight garrett frill cutter, make six frills. Cut each to a depth of 2 cm (1½ inches). Using a little egg white or gum arabic, stick around the edge of the cake card for the canopy frill. Make a feature of the join by lifting the corners slightly and cut more joins to even the spacing.

14 Roll out 75g (3oz) of the dark dusky pink modelling fondant and cut strips 1.5 cm (½ inch) in depth for around the top of the bed. Indent the rose pattern as before and stick in place using a little egg white or gum arabic. Stick a line of large gold beading around the bottom edge and a line of fine gold beading around the inside at the top.

15 Water down the pink, blue, yellow and mauve food colouring paste with a little water. Keeping the fine paintbrush quite dry, paint the mattresses

with the different colours to highlight the patterns.

16 With the light and dark dusky pink modelling fondant trimmings, model all the roses by rolling up flattened sausage shapes. Put six aside, then stick the remaining roses around the bottom of the bed.

17 To make the princess, model the skirt first in a kneeling position using 75g (3oz) of the white modelling fondant. With the remaining white modelling fondant, make her bodice, her crown, two sleeves, and roll out and cut a heart shape for her collar using the small heart cutter.

18 Using the flesh modelling fondant, roll a ball for her head, a tiny nose, and model her hands and feet. Mark her open mouth with the tip of the No. 3 piping nozzle. Model her two eyes, using some of the white trimmings. Stick everything together, using a little egg white or gum arabic. If necessary, use pieces of foam for support whilst drying. Stick the roses in place, tumbling down her dress.

19 Colour some of the white trimmings a bright green and roll a tiny ball for the pea. Position the pea in the princess's open hand.

20 Using the cream royal icing and No. 3 piping nozzle, pipe her hair cascading down her back. Leave the cake to dry for at least 8 hours, or overnight.

21 Draw the princess's eyes, using the blue and black food colouring pens. Dust a little pink dusting powder on to her cheeks to give her a slight blush.

22 Apply the edible gold leaf to her crown following the manufacturer's instructions.

Right: The Princess and the Pea

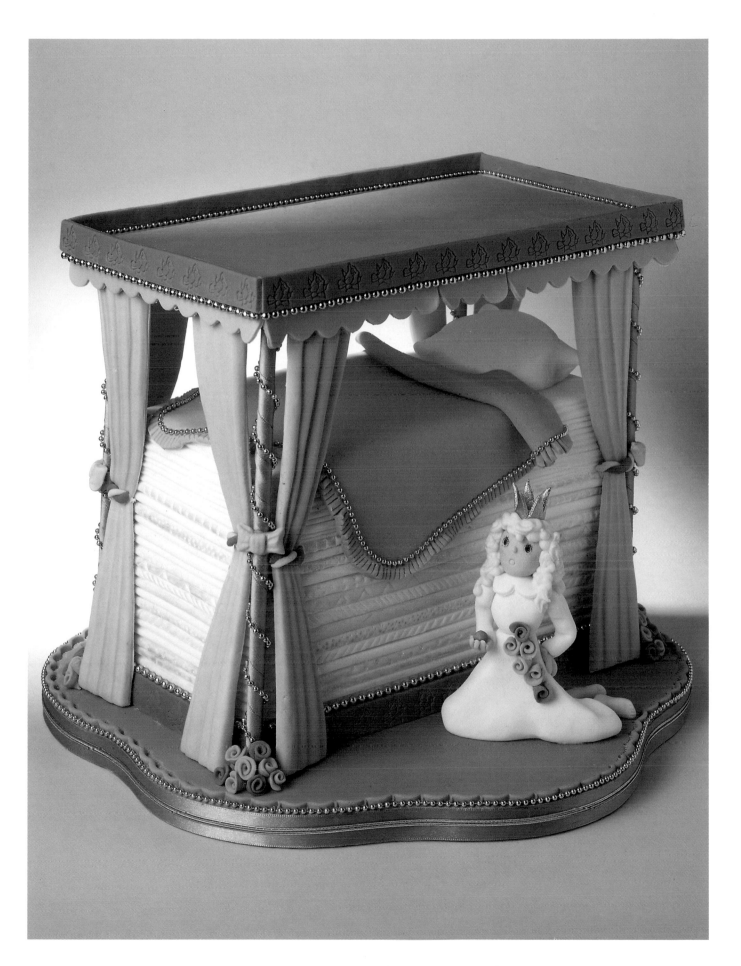

The Three Little Pigs

Then the wolf said
"I'll huff and I'll puff and I'll blow your house in"

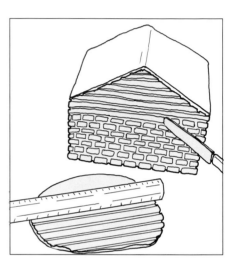

You will need:

1 Madeira cake (size 5)
1.500kg (3lb 6oz) fondant icing
green, golden brown, cream, black,
   red, dark brown, blue, pink and
   yellow food colouring paste
600g (1lb 5oz) butter cream
egg white or gum arabic
475g (1lb 2¹/₄oz) modelling fondant
red dusting powder
black and red food colouring pens

Equipment:

25 cm (10 inch) hexagonal cake
   board
cocktail sticks
ruler
fine paintbrush

Colour:

Fondant icing: 350g (12oz) green,
   750g (1lb 11oz) golden brown,
   75g (3oz) cream, 25g (1oz) black,
   300g (11oz) rust (red with a
   touch of dark brown)
Modelling fondant: 25g (1oz) red,
   225g (8oz) dark brown, 25g (1oz)
   blue, 75g (3oz) pale pink, 50g
   (2oz) yellow, 50g (2oz) dark grey,
   5g (¹/₄oz) dark pink, 5g (¹/₄oz)
   white, 10g (¹/₂oz) pale grey,
   5g (¹/₄oz) black

1 Cover the cake board with the green fondant icing and put aside to dry.

2 Slice the top off the cake so it is completely flat. Cut the cake in half, then cut a 7 cm (3 inch) strip from the length of each cake, so you are left with four cakes, two measuring 12 x 18 cm (5 x 7 inches) and two measuring 7 x 12 cm (3 x 5 inches).

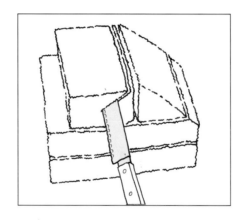

3 Put the two larger cakes one on top of the other, then put the two smaller cakes side by side, centrally on the top. The join should run along the shorter length. Using the join at the top as a guide, slice from the join sloping downwards to the top of the second layer, taking off the edge. Repeat for the other side to make the pointed roof.

4 Put aside 75g (3oz) of the butter cream for the chimney later. Sandwich the layers of the house together using half of the butter cream, then with the remaining butter cream, spread a thin layer over the surface of the cake to help the fondant icing stick.

5 Roll out one third of the golden brown fondant icing. Mark the lines across for the bricks using a ruler, then cut the bottom straight. Carefully turn the fondant icing over and place the back of the cake down on to it, lining up the straight edge at the bottom. Trim to fit. Put the house upright and use a knife to mark the vertical lines for each brick. Cover the front of the house in the same way using half of the remaining golden brown fondant icing. Position the cake on the cake board. Cover the two sides of the house by measuring and cutting pieces to fit, using the remaining golden brown fondant icing. Reserve the trimmings.

6 To make room for the door, cut out a piece of cake from the front of the house measuring 5 x 7 cm (2 x 3 inches) and cut in to a depth of 2.5 cm (1 inch). To make the chimney, cut this piece of cake in half then put one on top of the other. Cut a slight 'v' into the base so it will fit on the roof.

Right: Detail of wolf.

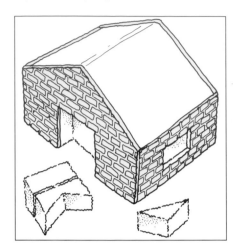

7 Using the reserved butter cream, sandwich the layer together and stick the chimney in place, then spread a thin layer of butter cream over the surface of the chimney and around the door area at the front to help the fondant icing stick. With the golden brown fondant icing trimmings, cover the chimney as before by measuring and cutting pieces to fit.

8 Cut an oblong measuring 6 x 5 cm (2½ x 2 inches) in the side of the house for the window, taking out just the fondant icing.

9 Using half of the cream fondant icing, model little flat stones in different sizes and arrange round the door area. Model the four stepping stones for the pathway. With the remaining cream fondant, make the door step and press down on the centre to make a slight dip. Position the pathway and the doorstep on the cake board.

10 Cover the window area and top of the chimney with the black fondant.

11 Using the red modelling fondant, make the arch-shaped front door and mark the lines with a knife. Lift the arch-shaped fondant carefully to prevent the marked lines stretching and put in place, sticking with a little egg white or gum arabic.

12 To make the porch roof, thickly roll out 50g (2oz) of the dark brown modelling fondant and cut a triangular shape 5 cm (2 inches) in width. Mark the wood lines with a ruler and the woodgrain pattern with a cocktail stick. With 25g (1oz), make the two porch stands, marking the woodgrain pattern as before. Put aside to dry.

13 With a 50g (2oz) piece of the dark brown modelling fondant, roll five sausage shapes, four for the corner posts and one for the windowsill, marking the woodgrain as before. Stick all the pieces in place, if necessary using a piece of foam to support the windowsill whilst drying.

14 To make the wooden straw shed, thickly roll out 75g (3oz) of the dark brown modelling fondant to a depth of 1.5 cm (½ inch) and cut an oblong measuring 5 x 4 cm (2 x 1½ inches). Trim out a space at the top for the straw. Using the trimmings, roll out and cut a roof, 4 cm (1½ inches) in width. Mark the wood lines and woodgrain as before and put aside to dry. Position the base of the wooden straw shed on the board.

15 With the remaining dark brown modelling fondant, roll out and cut a window shutter and make the wooden trims for around the top of the chimney and just under the roof, marking the woodgrain as before. With the trimmings, model four twigs, one for each corner of the chimney. Stick everything in place using a little egg white or gum arabic. Stick the porch stands to the porch roof, then stick the porch in position just above the front door.

16 Roll out the blue modelling fondant and cut out a window shutter as before. Roll out the trimmings paperthin and stick to the base of the wooden shutter making it look like paint. Reserve the trimmings for later.

17 To make the roof tiles, thickly roll out the rust fondant icing and cut oblong shapes, 2.5 cm (1 inch) in length. Press your finger on to the centre of each to indent it slightly. Cover the roof with the tiles starting at the bottom and building up line by line. Flick up the edges slightly to make them look a little uneven. Cover the porch roof, and with the trimmings, roll a sausage shape and position it on the top of the chimney, for the wolf to sit in.

18 To make the three little pigs, split 50g (2oz) of the pale pink modelling fondant into three equal pieces. Roll 3 balls for the heads. Using the remaining pale pink modelling fondant, model the three noses and six ears. Push the end of the paintbrush into each face to form the mouths and push downwards slightly to open up. Stick the noses in place and indent the nostrils with the end of the paintbrush. Stick each pig in the window using a little egg white.

19 Using three-quarters of the yellow modelling fondant, model the three hats and one kerchief. Mark the criss-cross pattern on the hats with a knife. With the red modelling fondant trimmings, model one kerchief and the paintbrush handle. With the green fondant icing trimmings, model another kerchief. Stick everything in place using a little egg white or gum arabic.

20 Model the wolf by rolling a cone shape with half of the dark grey modelling fondant. Push down on the centre to shape the face and nose. With the remaining dark grey modelling fondant, roll a ball for his body and flatten slightly, then model two paws and two ears. Stick everything in place in the centre of the chimney with the paws resting on top of the chimney. Mark the paws and his mouth with a cocktail stick.

21 With the dark pink modelling fondant make the wolf's tongue and the inside of his ears and stick in place.

22 Using the white modelling fondant, roll out and cut out the notice, marking each corner with the end of the paintbrush. Model the wolf's eyes and stick in place.

23 Make the wolf's hair, two eyebrows, the paint tin, a tiny handle and the paintbrush bristles using the pale grey modelling fondant. Put the tin handle to one side, then stick everything in place with a little egg white or gum arabic.

24 Using the black modelling fondant, make the eyes for the three little pigs and the wolf and model the wolf's nose, then stick in place.

25 Cut the remaining yellow modelling fondant into small squares and mark rough lines on them to make the straw. Stick on to the straw shed with the roof roof resting on top.

26 With the blue modelling fondant trimmings, model the paint on the paintbrush and the paint on top of the tin. Stick the tin handle in place.

27 Water down a little of the brown food colouring paste with 1 tablespoon of water. Using the fine paintbrush, paint a thin coat over all the 'wood' to highlight the woodgrain. Leave everything to dry for at least 8 hours, or overnight.

28 Rub a little of the red dusting powder on to some of the bricks with your finger.

29 With the black and red food colouring pens, draw 'MR WOLF KEEP OUT'.

Alternative design:

You could cover two more cake boards, one with flattened straw on it and the other with scattered wood, both made from modelling fondant. Put them in order on the birthday party table to tell the story of the three little pigs.

Little Red Riding Hood

"Oh Grandma, what big eyes you ve got"
"All the better to see you with"

You will need:

1 Victoria sponge cake (size 2)
1.650kg (3lb 10oz) fondant icing
blue, cream, black, yellow, red, flesh
   and brown food colouring paste
425g (15oz) butter cream
egg white or gum arabic
565g (1lb 4¹/₂oz) modelling fondant
50g (2oz) royal icing
red, green, yellow, blue and black
   food colouring pens

Equipment:

20 cm (8 inch) square cake card
ruler
scissors
6 flat-headed pins or strong non-
   toxic tape
25 cm (10 inch) square cake
   board
cocktail sticks
fine paintbrush
garrett frill cutter
no. 4 and no. 2 plain piping nozzles
foam pieces
crimping tool
waxed paper

Colour:

Fondant icing: 400g (14oz) blue,
   1.250kg (2lb 12oz) cream
Modelling fondant: 250g (9oz) grey
   (a touch of black), 50g (2oz)
   white, 125g (4oz) yellow, 25g
   (1oz) black, 15g (¹/₂oz) flesh, 75g
   (3oz) red, 25g (1oz) brown
Royal icing: 25g (1oz) black, 25g
   (1oz) cream

1 To make the back board that supports the bed canopy and curtains, mark the centre two inches on the top edge of the cake card, using a ruler. Draw two lines down from the measurement to the bottom two corners, then cut along each line.

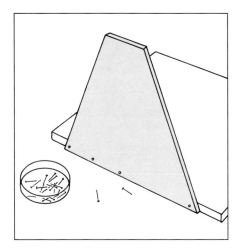

2 With the six flat-headed pins or the strong tape, attach the cake card to the back of the cake board, the widest part at the base.

3 Using 400g (14oz) of the blue fondant, cover the cake board and the cake card one at a time and trim to fit. Put aside to dry.

4 Slice the top off the cake to make it completely flat, then cut exactly in half. Trim 4 cm (1¹/₂ inches) from each length.

5 Sandwich one cake on top of the other, using half of the butter cream, then spread the remaining butter cream over the surface of the cake to help the fondant stick.

6 Thinly roll out 225g (8oz) of the cream fondant and use it to cover the bed completely. Put the cake on the cake board. The cake should be pushed up flush against the cake card.

7 Model the pillow, using a 75g (3oz) piece of the cream fondant, and then stick to the bed and cake card with a little egg white or gum arabic. With a 25g (1oz) piece, model the pelmet and then stick the pelmet on top of the cake card.

8 To make the bed valance, roll out 125g (4oz) of the cream fondant and from it cut a long thin strip, which should measure at least 53 x 4 cm (21 x 1¹/₂ inches). Roll the end of the paintbrush along the bottom edge to frill, then gently stick around the base of the bed.

9 Using 150g (5oz) of the grey modelling fondant, model the wolf's body, his head and two pointed ears. With the remaining grey modelling fondant, make his two legs for under the bed cover and his two bushy eyebrows. Put the ears, tail and eyebrows aside, then stick the wolf on to the bed with his arms crossed against his chest, using a little egg white or gum arabic. Cut the wolf's mouth open with a knife.

10 Using a 25g (1oz) piece of the white modelling fondant, make both the wolf's eyes and model grandma's hat. Stick the wolf's ears and eyebrows in place, on to the wolf already postioned on the bed.

11 Roll out 50g (2oz) of the yellow modelling fondant and cut out a shawl. Wrap around the wolf's shoulders.

12 To make the bed cover, roll out 375g (13oz) of the cream fondant and cut a 20 cm (8 inch) square. Trim at each corner to round off then lay over the wolf.

13 With 125g (4oz) of the cream fondant, make the frill for both the pillow and the bed cover, using the garrett frill cutter. Press a cocktail stick gently around each frill to indent the lines of the pattern.

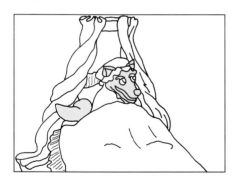

14 To make the curtains, roll out the remaining cream fondant and cut out two oblong shapes, each measuring 23 x 10 cm (9 x 4 inches). Gather up the top of each and stick in place with a little egg white or gum arabic. Stick the wolf's tail in place.

15 Using the blue fondant trimmings, make the two curtain tie-backs and tassels, stick in place. Mark the rope pattern and tassels with a knife.

16 To make Little Red Riding Hood, first model a triangle shape for her dress using a 75g (3oz) piece of the yellow modelling fondant. Leaving enough room for her legs and feet, stick to the edge of the bed, using a little egg white or gum arabic. If necessary, use a piece of foam for support whilst drying. With the yellow modelling fondant trimmings, roll two sausage shapes for sleeves and stick in place.

17 Cut out an apron for the front of her dress, using the remaining white modelling fondant and mark the pleats with a knife. With some of the trimmings, make four pointed teeth for the wolf's mouth. Stick everything in place with a little egg white or gum arabic.

18 With the black modelling fondant, model Red Riding Hood's legs and feet, the wolf's nose and two pupils for his eyes and stick in place.

19 Using the flesh modelling fondant, roll a ball for her head flattened slightly for her face, and a tiny ball for her nose. Indent her mouth with the No. 4 piping nozzle. Make her two hands.

20 To make the cloak, roll out 50g (2oz) of the red modelling fondant and cut a triangle shape 10 cm (4 inches in length). Trim the top straight and mark the pleats. Wrap around Little Red Riding Hood. Make a small bow with the trimmings and stick in position. Stick her head with her nose in place.

21 With the black royal icing and the No. 4 piping nozzle, pipe her hair. Keep it short at the back to leave room for the hood and pipe it long at the sides. Using the remaining red modelling fondant, model her hood and also the two slippers. Press the hood gently on to her head. Stick the slippers on to the cake board and make the fur with the yellow modelling fondant trimmings. Stick in place and indent with a cocktail stick.

22 To make the basket, roll 2 tiny sausage shapes with a little brown modelling fondant and twist together to make the handle. Leave to dry in a curve. Roll the remaining brown modelling fondant into a ball and flatten the top. Using the crimping tool, crimp sideways all around, then crimp a line for the top edge. Cut a 2.5 cm (1 inch) square for the napkin, using the white modelling fondant trimmings and position on the top of the basket. Put the basket on to the bed pushed up against Little Red Riding Hood's hand. Make her two eyes and stick in place.

23 With the cream royal icing and the No. 2 piping nozzle, pipe the dots on the cover and around the pillow.

24 Pipe the wolf's glasses on to the piece of waxed paper, using the remaining black royal icing and the No. 2 piping nozzle.

25 Using the food colouring pens, draw the pattern on the bedclothes, curtains and pelmet, Little Red Riding Hood's eyes and eyebrows, the flowers on her dress, the dots on the wolf's hat and the check pattern on the napkin.

26 Stick the handle on the basket using a little egg white or gum arabic.

27 Carefully peel the waxed paper away from the glasses and stick the glasses on the end of the wolf's nose. Using a knife, mark the lines on the wolf for his fur.

Rumpelstiltskin

*"Ah! How famous it is that nobody knows
That my name is Rumpelstiltskin"*

You will need:

5 Madeira cakes (size 1, size 2,
   size 3 and size 4)
1.985kg (4lb 5½oz) fondant icing
black, brown, green, mauve and
   flesh food colouring paste
400g (14oz) butter cream
egg white or gum arabic
black food colouring pen

Equipment:

25 cm (10 inch) square cake board
ruler
cocktail sticks
fine paintbrush
7 cm (4 inch) plain circle cutter
foam pieces
plastic skewer or dowelling
gold thread or curling ribbon

Colour:

Fondant icing: 350g (12oz) stone
   (black and brown kneaded
   together until streaky), 400g
   (14oz) green, 200g (7oz) brown,
   600g (1lb 5oz) mauve, 200g (7oz)
   pale flesh, 5g (¼oz) white, 5g
   (¼oz) black, 225g (8oz) grey

1 Cover the cake board with the stone-effect fondant. Using a ruler, mark the lines for the cell floor. Texture each stone by scratching with a knife and indenting with your fingers, then put aside to dry.

2 Slice the tops off all the cakes so that they are completely flat. Cut the mug cake into three equal slices, then cut one of the slices into quarters. Trim the remaining two slices to make oval shapes to use for the feet and trim off any angles.

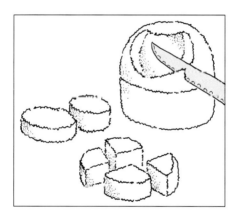

3 Place the large bowl cake on top of the 15 cm (6 inch) round cake. For the arms, make a cut about 1 cm (½ inch) deep, and continue to cut in a curving line down to the bottom of the bowl cake. Mark the back of the arm with a curving line 5 cm (2 inches) behind the first line. Repeat for the other arm.

4 Slice down the front, keeping the tummy area quite rounded, and trim round to the arms. Slice downwards at the back, keeping the bottom area rounded, then trim round to the arms.

5 Slice out a piece of cake directly underneath each arm, then trim the base of the cake by about 5 mm (¼ inch) all the way round, cutting at an inward angle. Trim the edges off the arms and trim any angles left round the cake.

6 Sandwich the two cakes together with 125g (4oz) of the butter cream, then place on the cake board.

7 To make the head, put the two small bowl cakes together and trim the front almost flat to shape the face. Sandwich together with some of the butter cream.

8 Stick the two feet in position with a little butter cream, then stick one of the small cake quarters on top of each foot for the legs, the right angle forming the knees.

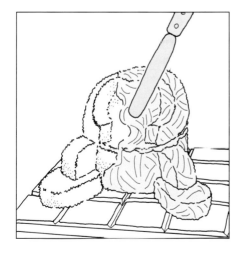

9 Using a spatula or other flat blunt knife spread a thin layer of butter cream all over each cake to help the fondant stick.

10 To make Rumpelstiltskin's leggings, roll out 400g (14oz) of the green fondant and cut an oblong measuring 50 x 7 cm (20 x 3 inches). Roll the fondant up, and keeping the join at the back, unroll around the base of the cake. Trim around the feet and rub the join closed with your fingers. Smooth the top of the leggings in line with the surface of the cake to remove the ridge.

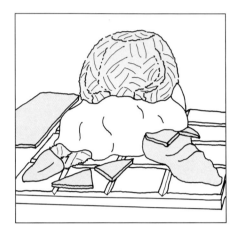

11 Split a 50g (2oz) piece of the brown fondant exactly in half and pad out each toe to a point. Roll out the remaining brown fondant, cut in half and cover each shoe completely. Indent with your fingers to make the creases. With the trimmings, cut out the shoe flaps and stick in place with a little egg white or gum arabic.

12 To make the jacket, roll out 375g (13oz) of the mauve fondant and then cut an oblong measuring 32 x 12 cm (13 x 5 inches). Carefully roll up the fondant then, keeping the join at the front for the jacket opening, unroll the fondant around the top of the cake. Trim at the front to make a neat join and smooth the fondant around the arms and upwards around the shoulders. Cut away any excess fondant from the top. Using the fondant trimmings, roll out and cut a circle for the collar, using the circle cutter. Make small cuts all round the edge of the collar and around the bottom of the jacket, then position the collar on top of the cake.

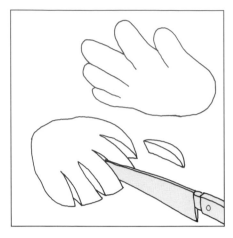

13 To make the hands, cut a 75g (3oz) piece of the pale flesh fondant exactly in half. Roll into two balls and then flatten slightly. Make the cuts for the fingers with a knife and smooth out the edges. Stick in place with just a little egg white or gum arabic, using pieces of foam for support whilst drying, if necessary.

14 Using 25g (1oz) of the mauve fondant, roll out and cut the two cuffs. Make small cuts along one edge, then stick the cuffs in place over the hands.

15 Using 15g (½oz) of the pale flesh fondant, roll two small balls to pad out the cheeks and model a long nose. Press each in position on the face. Roll out the remaining pale flesh fondant and cover the face completely, smoothing the fondant around the sides in line with the surface of the cake. Model a tiny wart, stick on the end of his nose.

16 Position Rumpelstiltskin's head on his body and push the skewer or dowelling down through the top of the head to keep it firmly in place.

17 Using a cocktail stick, mark the smile and the laughter lines around the eyes. Smooth the eye area and the bridge of his nose with your fingers to shape. With a tiny amount of white fondant, model the two eyes. Model the iris with some of the brown fondant trimmings and the pupils with the black fondant and stick in place with a little egg white or gum arabic. Stick a tiny amount of white fondant on to the eyes to give a sparkle.

18 Model Rumpelstiltskin's beard using 75g (3oz) of the grey fondant. Stick in place, pinching and pulling with your fingers to shape. With 25g (1oz), model his moustache and two eyebrows. Thickly roll out the remaining grey fondant and cover the top and back of his head for his hair. Pinch and pull the fondant down and around his face. Using a little egg white or gum arabic, stick his moustache and eyebrows in place.

19 To make Rumpelstiltskin's hat, thickly roll out a 75g (3oz) piece of the mauve fondant and model an oval shape. With the remaining mauve fondant, roll a sausage shape, tapering it in at one end and flattening slightly. Stick on top of the hat, letting the thinner end fall to one side. Smooth the top with your hands to round off. Leave the cake to dry for at least 8 hours, or overnight.

20 Using the black food colouring pen, draw Rumpelstiltskin's eyelashes. Position the gold thread or curling ribbon in his hands and around the cake, to represent the straw that was spun to gold.

Right: Rumpelstiltskin

Cinderella

Cinderella's step-mother said "You cannot go to the ball with us, for you have no clothes"

You will need:

2 Pink marble cakes (size 1)

1.250kg (2lb 12oz) fondant icing

navy blue, yellow, pink, flesh, cream, black and mauve food colouring paste

250g (9oz) butter cream

150g (6oz) modelling fondant

sugar glue

275g (10oz) simple pastillage

25g (1oz) royal icing

green dusting powder

pink and white edible sparkle powder

brilliant silver lustre powder

$\frac{1}{2}$ teaspoon granulated sugar

blue and black food colouring pens

Equipment:

30 cm (12 inch) oval cake board

cocktail sticks

crimping tool

miniature bow cutter

fine and medium paintbrushes

7 cm (3 inch), 6 cm (2$\frac{1}{2}$ inch) and 5 cm (2 inch) plain circle cutters

large, medium and small calyx cutters

broderie anglaise eyelet cutter

small rose leaf cutter

dried bay leaf

foam sheet

small pieces of foam

small shell piping nozzle

Colour:

Fondant icing: 375g (13 oz) navy blue, 875g (1lb 15oz) white

Modelling fondant: 50g (2oz) white, 50g (2oz) pink, 10g ($\frac{1}{4}$oz) flesh, 25g (1oz) grey (a touch of black), 15g ($\frac{1}{2}$oz) pale mauve

Pastillage: 270g (9$\frac{3}{4}$oz) white, 5g ($\frac{1}{4}$oz) yellow

Royal icing: 25g (1oz) cream

1 Cover the cake board with 300g (11oz) of the navy blue fondant. Using the crimping tool, crimp around the edge of the board and put aside to allow to dry.

2 Slice the tops off each cake so they are completely flat.

3 To make the opening for the inside of the carriage, cut a strip from the centre of one cake measuring 5 cm (2 inches) in width. Make the cut 2 cm (1 inch) deep, then trim a further 1 cm ($\frac{1}{2}$ inch) into a point.

4 Roll out two-thirds of the remaining navy blue fondant. Using a little butter cream to stick in place, cover the recess and trim to fit. With the remaining navy

blue fondant, cut a strip measuring 5 x 15 cm (2 x 6 inches). Place on the centre of the second cake, using a little butter cream to stick and trim to fit at each end.

5 Sandwich the two cakes together using 75g (3oz) of the butter cream. With the remaining butter cream, spread a thin layer over the surface of the cake to help the fondant stick.

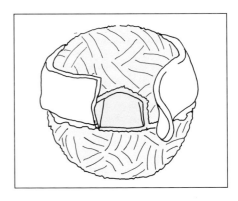

6 To give the carriage more shape, roll out 125g (4oz) of the white fondant into an oblong measuring 30 x 5 cm (12 x 2 inches). Cut in half, then wrap each piece around one half of the top half of the carriage and trim at each window. Smooth the fondant in line with the surface of the cake.

7 Thickly roll out the remaining white fondant and cover the cake completely, stretching the pleats and teasing the fondant in around the base. Push down into the top of the carriage with your thumb to indent. Using the blunt edge of a knife, mark even lines from top to bottom, then rub with your fingers to soften the line.

8 Cut out the two windows measuring 8 x 6 cm (3 x 2¹/₂ inches) either side of the carriage using the dents in the fondant icing as a guide. Cut out a small doorway 2.5 cm (1 inch) in length under the front carriage window.

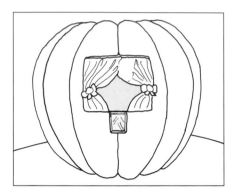

9 Using 50g (2oz) of white modelling fondant, make the curtains, marking the pleats with a cocktail stick. Arrange at the windows, sticking in place with a little sugar glue. Press the curtain flat where Cinderella's head will be. Reserve the white modelling paste trimmings for later.

10 Make the four chassis pieces using a 15g (¹/₂oz) piece of the white pastillage for each. Roll a sausage shape with one end rolled thinner. Roll to a length of 20 cm (8 inches) for the front end of the carriage and 23 cm (9 inches) for the back. Curl the thicker end of each round making a slight spiral, leave to dry on the foam sheet. The two seat cushions are made with a 50g (2oz) piece of the white pastillage. Cut exactly in half and model the cushions with two buttons for the centre and mark the pleats with the end of the paintbrush.

11 Make the wheels of the carriage using 75g (3oz) of the white pastillage. Use the 7cm (3 inch) circle cutter for the two larger back wheels and the inner circle cut from the 6 cm (2¹/₂ inch) circle cutter. For the two smaller front wheels, use the 6 cm (2¹/₂ inch) circle cutter for the outside and the 5 cm (2 inch) for the inside. Roll eight balls, four small and four tiny for the wheel bolts. Stick the four tiny balls on the centre of the larger balls and put aside.

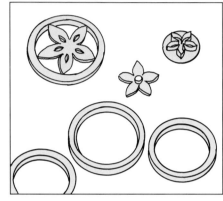

12 Using the large calyx cutter, cut two flower shapes, one at a time, for the larger wheels. Cut out the design in each, using the broderie anglaise eyelet cutter. If you don't have a cutter make the pattern with a large plain piping nozzle. Cut two more, using the medium calyx cutter, for the smaller wheels, again cutting the design with the eyelet cutter. Using the small calyx cutter, cut four flower shapes for each wheel. Stick the wheel bolts on the centre using a little sugar glue. Assemble the wheel together, sticking with sugar glue, and leave to dry on the foam sheet.

13 With the remaining white pastillage, model the seven curled stems, two small teardrop shapes, three teardrop shapes for the plume on the top of the carriage. Roll out and cut six leaves using the small rose leaf cutter and mark the leaf vein by pressing each leaf down on to the underside of the dried bayleaf. Roll out and cut five flower shapes using the small calyx

cutter. Cut each flower in half, then trim so both sides are even. Make a small step for the carriage door. Using the yellow pastillage, model the two small cone shapes, flattened at each end, for the inside of the two lanterns. Model the top and base with the white pastillage trimmings and cut thin strips for around the lantern. Stick everything together using a little sugar glue and stick one each of the halved flower trims into the top of the lanterns, then place on the foam sheet to dry.

14 To make Cinderella, model her skirt, bodice and two sleeves, using half of the pink modelling fondant. Make her skirt first and stick in place pressing into the doorway, marking the pleats with a cocktail stick. Stick her bodice in position just inside the window, then stick her arms in place, again marking the pleats with a cocktail stick. With the remaining pink modelling fondant, model the cushion with a button in the centre and mark the pleats.

15 Using the flesh modelling fondant, make Cinderella's head, a tiny nose and her two hands. Stick her head to the top of the curtain, resting on her bodice, then stick her nose and hands in place. Mark her smile.

16 Pipe Cinderella's hair using the cream royal icing and the piping nozzle. Paint her eyebrows.

17 With the remaining white modelling fondant, make Cinderella's eyes, her crown, her slipper and the cushion edging and tassels, marking the pattern with a knife. Stick everything in place with a little sugar glue.

18 Using the pink modelling fondant trimmings, make two bows, using the miniature bow cutter, four ears and two tiny noses for the mice and put aside. Twist some of the pink and white modelling fondant trimmings together for the curtain tie-backs, stick in place.

23 Mix the silver lustre powder with a little water to make a paste. Using the fine paintbrush, paint a thin layer over the centre of each wheel, Cinderella's crown, the window trims, the two lanterns and the crimped edging around the cake board. Leave to dry, then paint on a further thin coat.

24 To make Cinderella's dress and slipper sparkle, paint on a thin coat of sugar glue and sprinkle on the granulated sugar.

25 Using the medium paintbrush, dust the white sparkle powder over the cake to make it twinkle under light. Leave to dry for at least 8 hours, or overnight, with the chassis and wheels still supported.

26 Using the food colouring pens, draw the eyes on the mice and Cinderella.

Above: Cinderella in her carriage

19 To make the mice, roll two cone shapes for their bodies, using half of the grey modelling fondant. With the remaining grey modelling fondant make two heads, four hands, four feet and two long tails. Using the mauve modelling fondant, make the sleeves for each mouse and cut out two jackets and two collars. Assemble the mice together in their poses, sticking in place on the carriage seat cushions.

20 Leave everything to dry for at least 8 hours, or overnight.

21 When all the pastillage pieces are dry, assemble the carriage. Using the sugar glue, stick the four spiral chassis in place, the two longer pieces at the back of the carriage. Use pieces of foam for support whilst drying. Stick the cushions with the mice on top in position, resting on the chassis. Stick the plume on top of the carriage, the two lanterns in place, the two teardrop shapes on the back of the carriage, the doorway step, the halved flower trims around the window, the curly stalks resting on the cake board and the wheels stuck against the carriage. Put pieces of foam against each wheel to support them whilst drying. Dust the leaves with just a little of the green dusting powder and arrange around the cake.

22 Using the medium paintbrush, dust a little pink sparkle powder over the curtains and cushion seats to give them a little colour.

Goldilocks and The Three Bears

"Someone's been eating my porridge,"
said Father Bear

YOU WILL NEED:
1 Victoria sponge cake (size 3)
950g (2lb 1oz) fondant icing
yellow, red, green, blue, black, flesh
   and cream food colouring paste
375g (13oz) butter cream
475g (1lb 1oz) modelling fondant
egg white or gum arabic
brilliant silver lustre powder
red, green, blue and black food
   colouring pens
red dusting powder
175g (6oz) royal icing

EQUIPMENT:
30cm (12 inch) round cake board
cocktail sticks
crimping tool
5 cm (2 inch), 7 cm (2½ inch) plain
   circle cutters
heart cutter
blossom cutter
fine paintbrush
foam sheet
foam pieces
no. 3 plain piping nozzle
small shell piping nozzle

COLOUR:
Fondant icing: 375g (13oz) yellow,
   575g (1lb 4oz) white
Modelling fondant: 75g (3oz) red,
   25g (1oz) green, 125g (4oz) blue,
   125g (4oz) black, 75g (3oz) white,
   50g (2oz) flesh
Royal icing: 125g (4oz) cream, 50g
   (2oz) yellow

1 Cover the cake board with the yellow fondant. Using a knife make even cuts all round the edge to create the frill. Crimp a line following the frill, using the crimping tool.

2 Slice the top off the cake where it has risen to make it completely flat.

3 Slice a layer in the cake and sandwich back together using 225g (8oz) of the butter cream. Position the cake on the cake board, leaving room on one side for Goldilocks. With the remaining butter cream, spread a thin layer over the surface of the cake to help the fondant stick.

4 To cover the table, roll out 400g (14oz) of the white fondant. Place the cake board on to the fondant and cut around it. Lift the cake board off the fondant then place the circle over the cake, encouraging the pleats around the edge for the tablecloth.

5 For the square tablecloth, roll out the remaining white fondant, cut a 20 cm (8 inch) square. Position on the table.

6 To make baby bear's chair, roll out half of the red modelling fondant and cut a circle using the 5 cm (2 inch) circle cutter. Trim the bottom and sides of the circle to make the seat. Make the back of the chair in the same way and cut a heart in the centre, using the small heart cutter. Put aside 15g (½oz) of the red modelling fondant, then with the remaining piece, make four legs and two back rest posts.

7 Using all the green and 25g (1oz) of the blue modelling fondant, make daddy bear's and mummy bear's chair backs as before, but use the 7 cm (2½ inch) circle cutter. Cut out hearts in the green chair and flowers in the blue chair, using the heart shape and blossom cutters to create the shapes.

8 Using the black modelling fondant, make Goldilocks' two shoes, the porridge pot handle and four legs, then roll a ball with the remainder and model the pot. Put the shoes aside to dry, then stick the porridge pot together, using a little egg white or gum arabic.

9 With 50g (2oz) of the white modelling fondant, make the three bowls and spoons, all in slightly different sizes. Mix a little silver lustre powder with some water to make a paste. Using the fine paintbrush, paint a thin coat over the spoons, leave to dry for 10 minutes, then paint on a further thin coat.

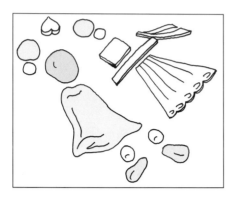

10 To make Golidlocks, model her two sleeves and her skirt, using the remaining blue modelling fondant. Pinch around the bottom of her skirt to make it flare out. Mark the sleeve pleats with a cocktail stick. With the remaining red modelling fondant, make her bodice. Using 15g (¹/₂oz) of the white modelling fondant, make Goldilocks' socks, sleeve edging, collar and apron. Pinch along the bottom edge of the apron to frill and mark the pleats with a cocktail stick. Stick the bodice to the skirt, then stick the sleeves and apron in place. Use pieces of foam for support whilst drying.

11 Make Goldilocks' head, tiny nose, two hands and legs with the flesh modelling fondant and stick in place, using a little egg white or gum arabic, again using pieces of foam for support. Mark her mouth with the tip of the No. 3 piping nozzle. With the remaining white modelling fondant, roll small balls and stick underneath her skirt for her petticoat. Stick her socks and shoes in place.

12 Put all the modelled pieces on to the foam sheet and leave with the cake to dry for at least 24 hours.

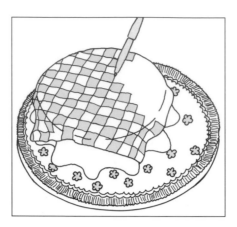

13 Using the red food colouring pen, draw the flowers on the cake board, the check tablecloth and the stripes on baby bear's bowl. With the green food colouring pen, draw each flower centre and all the leaves on the cake board, and the stripes on daddy bear's bowl. Draw the stripes on mummy bear's bowl using the blue food colouring pen. Draw both Goldilocks' eyes and eyebrows using the black food colouring pen. Dust a little red dusting powder on to her cheeks to give her a slight blush.

14 With the cream royal icing and the No. 3 piping nozzle, stick all the chair backs in position. Stick the porridge pot and the bowls in place and pipe some cream royal icing into each for the porridge. Stick the spoons in place with some cream royal icing piped over them.

15 Position Goldilocks on the cake board, sticking with a dab of royal icing.

16 With the yellow royal icing and the small shell piping nozzle, pipe Goldilocks' hair. Pipe in a circular motion to make the ringlets.

Alternative design:

Instead of Goldilocks you could make Daddy, Mummy and Baby Bear coming home for breakfast. Colour 250g (8oz) modelling fondant brown. Use 125g (4oz) to make Daddy Bear, 75g (3oz) to make Mummy Bear and the remaining piece to make Baby Bear. Assemble them together resting against the table for support. Perhaps with some brightly coloured modelling fondant you could make some clothes for them.

The Ugly Duckling

*He looked at his reflection in the water and saw he had,
indeed grown into a beautiful swan*

YOU WILL NEED:

2 Quick mix cakes (size 3)
1.300kg (2lb 14oz) fondant icing
orange, red, black and green food
  colouring paste
350g (12oz) butter cream
250g (9oz) modelling fondant
egg white or gum arabic

EQUIPMENT:

30 cm (12 inch) oval cake board
cocktail sticks
fine paintbrush

COLOUR:

Fondant icing: 350g (12oz)
  orange/red (equal amounts of
  orange and red), 950g (2lb 2oz)
  white
Modelling fondant: 25g (1oz) black,
  125g (4oz) grey, 50g (2oz)
  orange, 25g (1oz) green, 25g
  (1oz) white

1 Cover the cake board with the orange/red fondant icing and put aside to dry.

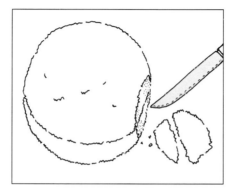

2 Slice the top off each cake so they are completely flat. Put the two cakes together, one on top of the other, and trim a small amount of cake from one side, so the cake will sit on the cake board without rolling.

3 Sandwich the two cakes together using 200g (7oz) of the butter cream and turn the cake into position. Using the remaining butter cream, spread a thin layer over the surface of the cake to help the fondant icing stick.

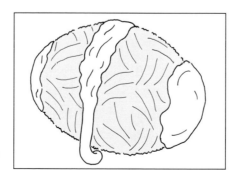

4 Split 150g (5oz) of the white fondant icing into two equal pieces and 'pad' out either end of the cake to make it more of an egg shape. Roll a long sausage with 75g (3oz), flatten slightly and place along the join. Press in line with the surface of the cake to seal the two cakes together.

5 Roll out the remaining white fondant icing and cover the cake completely, teasing the fondant icing in around the base by stretching the pleats outwards and smoothing downwards with your hands. Position the cake on the cake board.

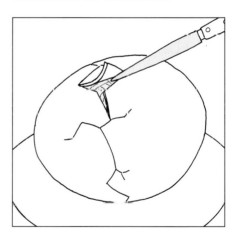

6 To make the crack in the shell, cut out a piece of fondant icing at the top of the cake and mark the lines for the crack down the sides. Fill the opening at the top with the black modelling fondant and then reserve all the trimmings for use later.

7 Model the Ugly Duckling's head using the grey modelling fondant and stick in place using a little egg white or gum arabic. Flick up a little fondant icing at the top of his head for his hair, using a knife.

8 With a tiny amount of the red fondant trimmings, model a ladybird. Indent the line on her back with a knife. Stick in place on the side of the shell with a little egg white or gum arabic.

9 Model the Ugly Duckling's beak using a 15g (½oz) piece of the orange modelling fondant and mark his smile with a knife. Stick in place and push the end of the paintbrush into the top of the beak to mark the holes.

10 Divide the green modelling fondant into six equal pieces and model all the leaves. Mark the centre vein with a knife and leave to dry.

11 Split the remaining orange modelling fondant into three equal pieces and make the flowers. Make a cone shape and push your finger into the larger end, remove, then carefully make five cuts around the edge for the petals. Pinch and pull each petal to shape and leave to dry upside down.

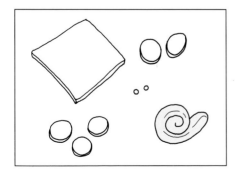

12 Using the white modelling fondant, make the piece of shell, the Ugly Duckling's eyes, the ladybird's eyes, the

three flower centres and the snail. For the snail, mix a tiny amount of the orange modelling fondant trimmings with the white until streaky. With this modelling fondant roll a long sausage shape then roll it up tightly leaving the end free for the head.

13 With the black modelling fondant trimmings, make the ladybird's face and her spots, two pupils for her eyes, two for the Ugly Duckling's eyes, and two for the snail's eyes. Put a 'sparkle' in the Ugly Duckling's eyes by sticking a tiny amount of white fondant on to each. Stick everything in place using just a little egg white or gum arabic and then leave the cake to dry for at least 8 hours, or overnight.

Alternative design:

To make a nest for the egg to sit in, roll a long thick sausage shape with 300g (10oz) of brown coloured fondant and position around the egg. Break chocolate flakes into long, thin pieces and build up around the egg pressing into the fondant for the twigs. To make it even prettier perhaps a few sugar daisies and leaves could be entwined.

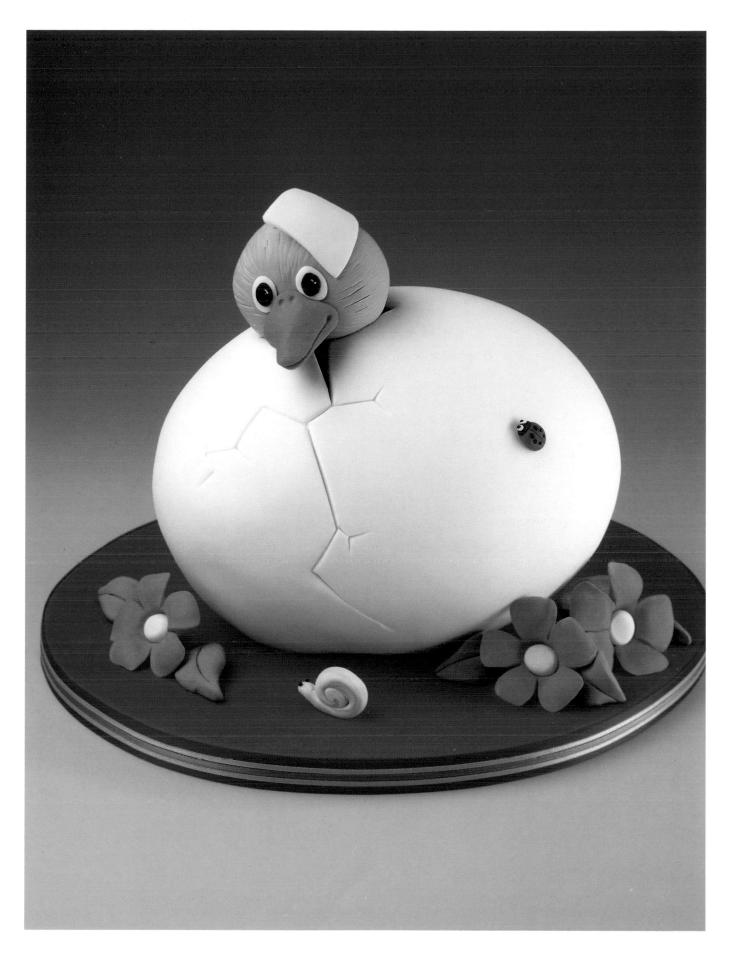

Little Jack Horner

....

Little Jack Horner sat in the corner
Eating a Christmas pie

You WILL NEED:

5 Madeira cakes (size 1, size 2,
   size 3 and size 4)
1.800kg (3lb 15oz) fondant icing
400g (14oz) butter cream
red, flesh, navy blue, black, cream
   and brown food colouring paste
egg white or gum arabic
225g (8oz) royal icing
red dusting powder
black food colouring pen

EQUIPMENT:

25 cm (10 inch) round cake board
crimping tool
cocktail sticks
fine paintbrush
plastic skewer or dowelling
8 cm (3 inch), 10 cm (4 inch) plain
   circle cutters
small holly leaf cutter
35 cm (14 inch) ribbon (excluding
   cake board)
no. 22 basket weave piping nozzle

COLOUR:

Fondant icing: 475g (1lb 1oz) white,
   825g (1lb 12oz) red, 200g (7oz)
   flesh, 225g (8oz) navy blue, 75g
   (3oz) light brown
Royal icing: 225g (8oz) cream

1 Roll out 250g (9oz) of the white fondant and cover the cake board completely. Using the crimping tool, crimp a line all around the edge of the cake board to create a border, and put aside to dry.

2 Slice the tops off all the cakes so they are completely flat.

3 Place the large bowl cake on top of the 15 cm (6 inch) round cake. To mark the arms, make a cut about 1 cm (¹/₂ inch) deep, and continue to cut in a curving line down to the bottom of the bowl cake. Mark the back of the arm with a similar curving line 5 cm 2 inches) behind the first line. Repeat for the other arm, but make the curve slightly higher.

4 Slice down the front of Little Jack Horner, at an outward angle, remembering to keep the tummy area quite rounded, and trim round to the arms. Slice downwards at the back, keeping the bottom area rounded, then again trim round to the arms.

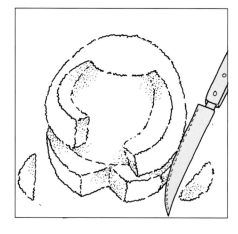

5 Slice out a piece of cake directly underneath each arm, then trim the base of the cake by about 5 mm (¹/₄ inch) all the way round, cutting at an inward angle. Trim out a small piece of cake at the front to separate the

two legs. Trim the edges off the arms and trim any angles left around the cake. Sandwich the two layers of the cake together using half of the butter cream and position on the centre of the cake board.

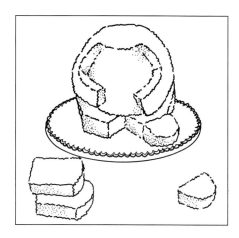

6 Cut the mug cake into three equal slices. Trim one of the slices into an oval shape then cut in half. Using a little butter cream, sandwich one each on to the cake for the beginning of Jack's legs. Trim the remaining slices to make two feet and put aside.

7 Put the two small bowl cakes together and trim the front slightly flat for the face. Sandwich the two cakes together using a little butter cream, then with the remaining butter cream, spread a thin layer over all of the cakes to help the fondant stick.

8 To lengthen the legs, split a 50g (2oz) piece of the white fondant in half and model two socks. Position on the cake board pushed up against the top of the legs.

9 To make the trousers, roll out 350g (12oz) of the red fondant and cut an oblong 9 x 25 cm (3¹/₂ x 17 inches). Wrap around the base of the cake, keeping the join at the back. Rub the join with your fingers to close. Trim around the hands and at the base, marking the pleat on the trousers with a knife. Smooth the top of the trousers in line with the cake to remove the ridge from the fondant.

10 Roll out 350g (12oz) of the red fondant and then cut an oblong measuring 20 x 38 cm (8 x 15 inches). Wrap around the top of the cake for the jacket, keep the join at the front for the opening. Trim at the bottom for the pleats.

11 Split a 5g (¹/₄oz) piece of the flesh fondant into three pieces. Pad out the face on the small round cake using one piece for Jack's nose and the other two pieces for his cheeks.

12 Roll out 125g (4oz) of the flesh fondant and cover the head completely, smoothing around the features with your hands. Don't worry if the back looks untidy as this will be covered with hair later. Cut out a smiling mouth with a knife and indent the bottom lip by smoothing with your finger. Position the head on to the body and push the skewer or dowelling down through the top to keep it in place.

13 Using 25g (1oz) of the flesh fondant for each, model the hands. Model the right hand with the thumb pointing up and stick both hands in position using a little egg white or gum arabic. With the remaining flesh fondant, make two small ears and put aside.

14 Model Jack's eyes with a small piece of white fondant. Knead together a small amount of the navy blue fondant with an equal amount of white for a paler blue and make the iris for his eyes. Colour a little white fondant black, then fill his mouth to give shadow and make the pupils for his eyes. Stick everything in place, then to give Jack a sparkle, stick two minute white dots on each pupil, using a little of the white fondant.

15 To make the hat rim, thickly roll out 75g (3oz) of the navy blue fondant and cut out a circle, using the 8 cm (3 inch) circle cutter. Position on top of Jack's head. With the trimmings, model six buttons. Stick two in place on the front of Jack's jacket, one on each of the trouser legs and put two aside.

16 Using the remaining navy blue fondant, roll out and cover both feet, tucking the fondant icing around for the front of each shoe. Stick in position, using a little egg white or gum arabic. Stick Jack's ears in place.

17 Make Little Jack Horner's collar and cuffs using 50g (2oz) of the white fondant. Pinch around the edge of the collar to make the frill. Cut each cuff with a point and stick in place with the buttons. Using some of the white fondant trimmings, stick a tiny strip into Jack's mouth for his teeth.

18 Using the remaining red fondant, model the top of Jack's hat. Stick the hat in place and then indent the folds with your finger.

19 Model the pie bowl with the remaining white fondant. Press around the side with your thumb to indent the pattern.

20 To make the pie crust, thickly roll out the light brown fondant and cut out a circle using the 10 cm (4 inch) circle cutter. Pinch around the edge to shape and stick on to the pie bowl. Cut out three holly leaves using the small holly leaf cutter and the light brown trimmings, and then arrange the leaves on the top of the pie.

21 Mix a little of the light brown, red and navy blue fondant trimmings together to make a dark plum colour. Stick a small piece on to the pie for the hole and then model the remaining piece into the shape of a plum. Push the plum carefully down on to Jack's thumb.

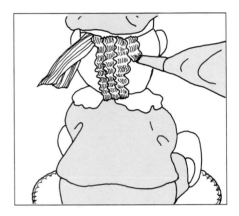

22 Pipe Jack's hair, using the cream royal icing and the piping nozzle. Pipe in wavy lines to curl. Fill the piping bag a little at a time to keep it manageable. Using half of the ribbon, fold and position on the back of Jack's head, piping hair over it to keep it in place. Make a bow with the remaining ribbon and stick on the front of the cake with a dab of royal icing.

23 Water down a little of the remaining cream royal icing and paint Jack's eyebrows using the fine paintbrush. Leave the cake to dry for at least 8 hours, or overnight.

24 Draw Jack's eyelashes with the black food colouring pen and rub a little red dusting powder on to his cheeks to give a blush.

Two Little Dicky Birds

Two little dicky birds sat on the wall
One called Peter, one called Paul

You will need:

1 Quick mix cake (size 1) or
  Victoria Sponge (size 1)
425g (15oz) butter cream
black, cream, brown, green, spruce
  green, pink, sky blue and yellow
  food colouring paste
1.250kg (2lb 12oz) fondant icing
275g (10oz) modelling fondant
egg white or gum arabic
black food colouring pen

Equipment:

30 cm (12 inch) oval cake board
cocktail sticks
fine paintbrush
large star nozzle
ruler
foam sheet
primrose cutter

Colour:

Fondant icing: 250g (9oz) grey, 250g
  (9oz) cream, 75g (3oz) light
  brown, 375g (13oz) mid-green,
  125g (4oz) light green, 175g (6 oz)
  spruce green
Modelling fondant: 150g (5oz) dark
  brown, 5g (¹/₆oz) grey, 15g (³/₄oz)
  pink, 75g (3oz) pale blue, 15g
  (³/₄oz) yellow

1 Slice the top off the cake so it is completely flat and trim each side to remove the crust.

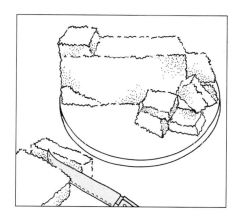

2 Cut the cake exactly in half and stand one half on its side on the centre of the cake board for the wall. Cut an oblong from the second half of the cake measuring 5 x 4 cm (2 x 1¹/₂ inches), 1 cm (¹/₂ inch) in depth and position on top of the wall at the front end to give a little height. Cut the remaining cake into uneven shapes and position the pieces at the far end of the wall on both sides, building up to make the bushes.

3 Using the butter cream, sandwich the shapes together and spread a thin layer over the entire cake to help the fondant stick.

4 Knead the grey, cream and light brown fondant together until you get a marbled effect. Put aside 150g (5oz) for later, then with the remaining marbled fondant icing model the stones in different sizes and position on the wall, building up from the base. Cover the wall completely with stones, leaving the top surface bare. Model six stones and then put them aside to allow them to dry out completely.

5 To make the large stones for the top, divide the remaining marbled fondant into ten equal pieces and roll thick sausage shapes. Position on top of the wall. Push down at each end to shape.

6 Using 275g (10oz) of the mid-green fondant icing, roll out a little at a time and stick to the surface of the cake board, using a little water. Push the tip of the large star nozzle into the fondant icing over and over to give the grass effect. With the remaining mid-green fondant, cover a piece of the cake at the front for a bush and another at the back. Push the end of the paintbrush into the bushes, twisting as you go, to give texture.

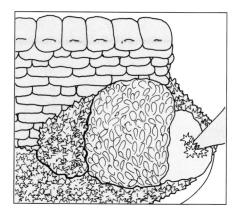

7 Make the remaining bushes as before, using the spruce green and light green fondant icing. To give a different type of texture, push the tip of the star nozzle into the fondant icing over and over again.

8 To make the end post and gate, split the dark brown modelling fondant into three equal pieces. With the first piece, model an end post measuring 10 cm (4 inches) in length and cut each end straight. Split the second piece in half and model two gate posts, each measuring 7 cm (3 inches) in length.

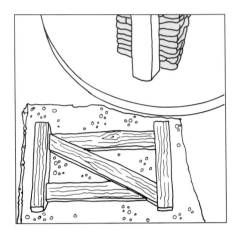

9 With the remaining piece of dark brown modelling fondant, roll out and cut three wooden planks, two measuring 9 cm (3½ inches) in length and the third measuring 12 cm (4½ inches). Trim the longer plank at each end to fit diagonally between the two gate posts. Using a knife, mark the lines for the woodgrain. Stick the end post in place and stick all the pieces for the gate together using a little egg white or gum arabic and leave to dry on a foam sheet.

10 With the grey modelling fondant, make the miniature mouse and put aside to dry.

11 Using the pink modelling fondant and the primrose cutter, make five flowers and indent the centre of each with the end of the paintbrush. With the trimmings, model two ears, a long tail and a tiny nose for the mouse and stick in place with a little egg white or gum arabic.

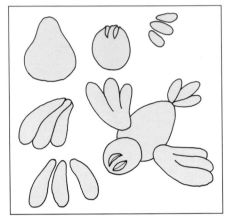

12 To make the two dicky birds, roll two 15g (¾oz) pieces of the pale blue modelling fondant into cone shapes for the two bodies. With the remaining pale blue modelling fondant, make the two heads, the four wings and two tail feathers. Using a knife, make small cuts on top of each head.

13 With the yellow modelling fondant, model five tiny flattened balls for the centre of each flower, a patch for the front of the sitting dicky bird, two beaks, and the two feet, marking each with a sharp knife.

14 Stick the birds, stones and flowers in place using a little egg white or gum arabic. Leave everything to dry for at least 8 hours, or overnight.

15 With the black food colouring pen draw the eyes and eyebrows on each dicky bird, the eyes and whiskers on the mouse and the smiley faces on the flowers.

16 Gently push the gate into the grass and stick to the end post, using a little egg white or gum arabic.

17 Water down a little of the brown food colouring paste with two teaspoons of water. Using a fine paintbrush, paint a thin coat over the surface of the end post and gate to highlight the woodgrain. Stick the mouse in place on the gatepost.

Alternative design:

To simplify the wall, instead of modelling separate stones, roll out the fondant and cover the wall part of the cake completely, then mark brick patterns with a knife. Perhaps you could colour the fondant a rich brown instead of grey.

Right: Two Little Dicky Birds

Jack and Jill

Jack and Jill went up the hill
To fetch a pail of water

You will need:

2 Pink marble cakes (size 3 and
  size 4)
925g (2lb) fondant icing
green, cream, black, brown, red,
  blue and yellow food colouring
  paste
525g (1lb 3oz) butter cream
300g (12oz) modelling fondant
sugar glue
125g (4oz) simple pastillage
75g (3oz) royal icing
1 tablespoon clear piping gel
black food colouring pen

Equipment:

32 cm (13 inch) oval cake board
large star nozzle
5 cm (2 inch) plain circle cutter
foam pieces
sheet of card

small rose petal cutter
clingfilm
no. 3 plain piping nozzle
small blossom plunger cutter

Colour:

Fondant icing: 350g (12oz) green,
  225g (8oz) cream, 350g (12oz)
  light green
Modelling fondant: 75g (3oz) grey (a
  touch of black), 50g (2oz) blue,
  50g (2oz) white, 50g (2oz) flesh,
  50g (2oz) yellow, 25g (1oz)
  brown
Pastillage: 75g (3oz) brown, 25g
  (1oz) rust (equal amounts of red
  and brown)
Royal icing: 25g (1oz) dark blue, 25g
  (1oz) brown, 25g (1oz) cream

1 Trim a little off the top of the large cake where it has risen to flatten slightly.

2 Cut the top edge from both of the cakes and put the smaller cake centrally on top of the other. Trim all around the cake at an angle to make the sloping hill shape. Position the cake on the cake board.

3 Spread half of the butter cream in the layer and sandwich back together. With remaining butter cream, spread a thin layer over the surface of the cake to help the fondant icing stick.

4 Using 225g (8oz) of the green fondant icing, roll a long sausage shape and wrap around the base of the cake, leaving a 10 cm (4 inch) gap at the front for the pathway. Smooth all the way around in line with the cake and the board edge.

5 Pad out the bottom of the path using a 75g (3oz) piece of the cream fondant icing and smooth in line with the cake and board. Using the remaining cream fondant icing, roll a long sausage shape thicker at one end and flatten slightly. Position down the front of the hill and smooth the edge to round off.

6 To cover the cake with grass, roll out rough shapes alternately with the remaining green and the light green fondant icing and cover the hill a little at a time. Press the tip of the large star nozzle into the fondant icing over and over to give a grass effect.

7 Dust the circle cutter with icing sugar and place on top of the hill as a guide for the stone well. Using the grey modelling fondant, model the stones for the base of the well and build up around the circle cutter, sticking in place with a little sugar glue. Roll out and cut a strip for the edge of the well 18 cm (7 inches) in length. Make the strip into a circle, sticking together with a little sugar glue. Mark the stones with a knife. Remove the circle cutter and stick the well edge on top.

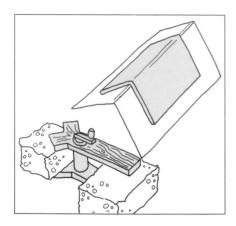

8 Make the top of the well using the brown pastillage. First roll out and cut the two stands 8 cm (3 inches) in length. Cut the top at an angle so the pointed roof will sit straight. Model the well handle. Make the rope holder for the centre measuring 3 cm (1½ inches) in length. Roll out the remaining brown pastillage and then cut out an oblong for the roof frame measuring 6 x 8 cm (2½ x 3 inches). Make a fold in the piece of card and lay the roof frame over the fold lengthways. When the pastillage has formed a crust, stick the well stand together using a little sugar glue and leave to dry using foam for support.

9 Using the rust pastillage and the small rose petal cutter, make all the tiles for the well roof. Roll the pastillage very thin and stick the tiles in place, building up from the bottom and letting each layer overlap. With the trimmings, roll a sausage shape for the top, stick in place and indent with a cocktail stick.

10 To make Jack and Jill, first model Jack's trousers using a 25g (1oz) piece of the blue modelling fondant. With 15g ½oz) of the blue modelling fondant, make Jill's top, her two shoes, a bow for her hat, and Jack's waistcoat. Cover with clingfilm to stop the pieces drying out before they are moved into position.

11 With the white modelling fondant, make Jack's top, two small flattened circles for his socks, Jill's hat, socks, bib and apron tie.

12 Put aside 15g (½oz) of the flesh modelling fondant, then with the remaining flesh modelling fondant model the two heads, four hands and two tiny noses.

13 Put aside 15g (½oz) of the yellow modelling fondant for later, then with the remaining yellow modelling fondant make Jill's skirt and her two puffed sleeves. Pinch around the bottom of the skirt to frill.

14 Using the brown modelling fondant, make Jack's cap, shoes and necktie and model the bucket, marking the lines with a knife.

15 Assemble Jack and Jill on the cake in their poses, sticking in place with a little sugar glue. Use pieces of foam for support whilst drying. Mark their open mouths with the tip of the piping nozzle.

16 Make the two little birds with the remaining blue modelling fondant. Cut two strips for the bucket and stick in place.

17 With the remaining yellow modelling fondant, make two beaks and a patch for the front of one bird and stick in place. Make all the flowers using the small blossom plunger cutter. Indent the centre of each to shape using the tip of the piping nozzle.

18 Leave the cake to dry for at least 8 hours, or overnight.

19 When everything is completely dry, position the well frame into the well, sticking it in place with a little sugar glue. Pipe the dark blue royal icing into the bottom of the well and around the frame, using the piping nozzle.

20 With the remaining flesh modelling fondant, roll a long thin sausage shape for the rope and indent with a knife. Cut a piece for the bucket and wrap the remaining rope around the centre of the well. Model the two knots for the bucket using the trimmings and stick everything in place.

21 For the water, put the clear piping gel into the bucket letting it fall over the grass. Don't be tempted to put some in the well as this could soften the well frame.

22 Using a little sugar glue, stick the roof on the well and the birds and flowers in place.

23 Draw the eyes on the two birds and on Jack and Jill using the black food colouring pen.

24 Pipe Jill's hair using the brown royal icing and the piping nozzle. Pipe in circles around her face to look like ringlets.

25 Using the cream royal icing and the piping nozzle, pipe Jack's hair.

Little Miss Muffet

Little Miss Muffet sat on her tuffet
Eating her curds and whey

You will need:

5 Madeira cakes (size 1, size 2, size 3, size 4)
1.975 kg (4lb 6oz) fondant icing
green, yellow, brown, flesh, chestnut, orange, blue, cream and black food colouring paste
375g (13oz) simple pastillage
egg white or sugar glue
450g (1lb) butter cream
315g (11¼oz) modelling fondant
75g (3oz) royal icing
black food colouring pen
edible green and white food paint
brilliant silver lustre powder
red dusting powder

Equipment:

30 cm (12 inch) oval petal-shaped cake board
cocktail sticks
small bowl
basketweave rolling pin
fine and medium paintbrushes
crimping tool
7 cm (3 inch) plain circle cutter
garrett frill cutter
no. 3 piping nozzle
plastic skewer or dowelling
piping bag
foam pieces

Colour:

Fondant icing: 350g (12oz) green, 275g (10oz) brown, 725g (1lb 10oz) white, 125g (4oz) flesh, 500g (1lb 2oz) chestnut
Pastillage: 125g (4oz) white, 250g (9oz) yellow
Modelling fondant: 75g (3oz) flesh, 5g (¼oz) orange, 75g (3oz) green, 25g (1oz) black, 25g (1oz) yellow, 75g (3oz) blue
Royal icing: 75g (3oz) cream

1 Cover the cake board with green fondant. Mark the lines, put aside to dry.

2 Dust the inside of the small bowl with icing sugar. Roll out the white pastillage and smooth into the inside of the bowl. Trim to even the rim. Leave for about 20 minutes to set, turn out and leave to dry.

3 To make the hat, roll out half of the yellow pastillage and cut out two 15 cm (6 inch) circles. Using the 7 cm (3 inch) circle cutter, cut out a circle in the centre of each. Print the basketweave pattern into each of the pastillage

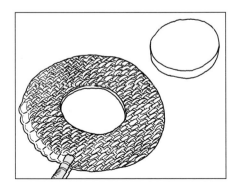

circles by pressing into them with the basketweave rolling pin. Using the egg white or sugar glue, stick the two hat rims together, back to back and crimp around the edge using a crimping tool.

4 Roll out the remaining yellow pastillage to a depth of 1 cm (½ inch) and cut out a circle using the 7 cm (3 inch) circle cutter. Print the basketweave pattern on the top and mark gently around the sides. Indent the underneath slightly so it will fit snugly. Leave to dry on a completely flat surface.

5 Make the cake tops flat. Place the large bowl cake on top of the round cake. For the arms, make a cut about 1 cm (½ inch) deep, continue to cut in a curve to the bottom of the bowl cake. Mark the back of the arm with a similar curving line 5 cm (2 inches) behind the first line. Repeat for the other arm.

6 Slice the front flat and trim round to the arms. Slice downwards at the back, keeping the bottom area rounded, then trim round to the arms. Cut out a piece of cake at the base to mark the two legs.

7 Slice out a piece of cake directly underneath each arm, then trim at the base of the cake by about 5 mm (¼ inch) all the way around, cutting at an inwards angle. Trim any edges or angles left.

8 Sandwich the two cakes together with ¼ of the butter cream and place on the cake board.

9 Cut the mug cake into three slices, cut one into two semi-circles. For the legs, cut the corners off each semi-circle and stick in place with a little butter cream. For the shoes, trim the other two circles into oval shapes, stick in place with butter cream.

10 Put the two small bowl cakes together and trim the front slightly flat to shape the face. Sandwich together, using the butter cream. Spread a thin layer of butter cream over the surface of the cakes to help the fondant stick.

11 Cut the brown fondant icing in half and cover the two feet for the shoes. Mark the heels with a knife. Reserve the trimmings for later.

12 Using 75g (3oz) of the white fondant, roll out and cut frills using the garrett frill cutter for the lacy petticoat. Press the tip of the No. 3 piping nozzle into the frill to make the holes. Stick the frills around the base of the cake.

13 Pad out the top of the sleeves with 50g (2oz) of the white fondant icing for each. Cut 25g (1oz) of the white fondant in half and pad out the base of the sleeves so each sleeve stands out.

14 For Little Miss Muffet's dress, roll out 500g (1lb 2oz) of the white fondant and cut out a circle 35 cm (14 inches) in diameter. Lift carefully and place over the top of the cake, pressing in the pleats under each arm. Mark the pleats on each sleeve with the end of a paintbrush. From the remaining white fondant, cut out a pinafore, marking the pleats with a cocktail stick. Make another frill as before and stick around the top edge of the pinafore. Model a large bow for the back and cut 3 straps, 2 for the shoulders and 1 for the waist-

band at the front of the pinafore. Stick everything in place with egg white or sugar glue. Reserve the trimmings.

15 Roll out the flesh fondant icing and cover the face completely. Position on top of the body and push the plastic skewer or dowelling through her head for support. With the trimmings, model a button nose, stick in place.

16 Cut the flesh modelling fondant in half and model the two hands. Stick in place with a little egg white or sugar glue and for extra support, make another frill as before using the white fondant and stick around each sleeve, letting the frill help hold the hands in place. Use pieces of foam for support. With the white fondant trimmings, model her 2 eyes and stick in place.

17 Place the 7 cm (3 inch) circle cutter on top of Little Miss Muffet's head as a guide for her hair. Divide the chestnut fondant icing into four equal pieces. With the first piece, model the hair for the back of her head with a parting in the centre marked with a knife and use egg white or sugar glue to stick it in place. Stick the second piece to the front of her head, pinching and pulling the fondant icing to 'curl'.

18 With the remaining two pieces, split each into three and roll long sausage shapes. Make two plaits and stick to her head. Mark some lines on the hair. With the chestnut fondant icing trimmings, model two irises for her eyes. Knead a tiny amount into some of the brown fondant icing trimmings and model her open mouth. Stick in place using a little egg white or sugar glue.

19 Model the two lips with the orange modelling fondant and stick in place.

20 Remove the circle cutter from the top of the head. Using a little egg white or sugar glue to stick, position the hat on her head.

21 Model two bows for the plaits using the green modelling fondant. Roll out and cut a strip 40 cm (16 inches) in length for the ribbon and stick in place.

22 Model the spider using the black modelling fondant. Roll two balls, one slightly larger than the other and model 8 legs and 2 pupils. Make 2 tiny balls for the eyes using the white fondant trimmings. Stick everything together using a little egg white or sugar glue. Make the 2 pupils for Little Miss Muffet and stick in place.

23 To make the curds and whey, cut the yellow modelling fondant into rough squares and place in the bowl. Using a piping bag without a nozzle, pipe the cream royal icing into the bowl. Leave to dry at a slight angle.

24 With the blue modelling fondant, roll out and cut a strip for the bowl and stick in place. With the remaining blue modelling fondant, model the spoon. Leave everything to dry for at least 8 hours, or overnight.

25 Using the black food colouring pen, draw Little Miss Muffet's eyelashes.

26 Using the white food paint and the fine paintbrush, paint two tiny dots on each of her eyes to give a sparkle.

27 Mix some of the green and white food paint together to make a pale green. Using the fine paintbrush, paint little squares over her dress.

28 Mix the silver lustre powder with a little water to make a thick paste. Paint a thin layer over the spoon using the medium paintbrush. Leave to dry, then paint on another thin coat.

29 Gently rub a little of the red dusting powder over Little Miss Muffet's cheeks to give her a slight blush.

Right: Little Miss Muffet

Little Boy Blue

Where is the boy who looks after the sheep?
He's under a haycock fast asleep

You will need:

1 Madeira cake (size 7)
450g (1lb) butter cream
1kg (2lb 4oz) fondant icing
yellow, blue, flesh, black, brown and
   pink food colouring paste
125g (4oz) modelling fondant
egg white or gum arabic
25g (1oz) royal icing
black food colouring pen
pink dusting powder

Equipment:

30 cm (12 inch) round cake board
cocktail sticks
clingfilm
3 cm (1½ inch) plain circle cutter
fine paintbrush
no. 3 piping nozzle

Colour:

Fondant icing: 1kg (2lb 4oz) yellow
Modelling fondant: 50g (2oz) blue,
   15g (½oz) white, 15g (½oz) flesh,
   15g (½oz) black, 5g (¼oz) grey,
   5g (¼oz) pink
Royal icing: 25g (1oz) brown

1 To make the cake more pointed, trim all round from the top down to 4 cm (1½ inches) from the base. Position on the cake board, towards the back. Trim the cuttings to fit all round the base and sandwich them in place with half of the butter cream.

2 With the remaining butter cream, spread a thin layer over the surface of the cake to help the fondant icing stick.

3 Thickly roll out the yellow fondant icing and cover the cake and board completely. Using a knife, mark the straw. Press quite deeply and make some 'criss-crosses'. To prevent the fondant icing drying out, cover the part you are not working on with clingfilm. Trim any excess from the edge of the cake board.

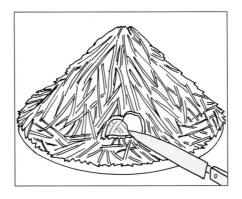

4 So that Little Boy Blue looks as if he is sinking into the haystack, cut out some fondant icing at the front, up to 6 cm (2½ inches) in height.

5 To make Little Boy Blue, roll a sausage shape with half of the blue modelling fondant, flatten slightly and make a cut to separate the two legs. Smooth the edges. Trim at the waist and the bottom of each leg. Model the horn with the trimmings. Using the remaining blue modelling fondant, roll a ball and flatten slightly. Cut the two arms either side and pinch around the base to frill out. Press the trousers and jacket in place at the base of the haystack. Using a knife mark the line down the front of the jacket and the crease lines around the waist.

6 Using the white modelling fondant, make the two socks, five buttons and two cuffs and roll out and cut a circle using the 3 cm (1½ inch) plain circle cutter for the collar.

7 Model the head, nose and two hands, using the flesh modelling fondant.

8 Model the boots and roll a thin sausage for the belt, using the black modelling fondant. Stick everything in position, using egg white or gum arabic.

9 Mark the mouth with the tip of the piping nozzle and draw the closed eyes with a cocktail stick. Pipe the curly hair using the brown royal icing.

10 With some of the yellow fondant trimmings, make extra straw, position around Little Boy Blue to fill any gaps.

11 Make the mice, using the grey modelling fondant. For the tails and paws, make holes in the straw and push each gently in place. Mark the smiles and paws with a knife. Model tiny noses using the pink modelling fondant and stick everything in position using a little egg white or gum arabic.

12 Leave the cake to dry for at least 8 hours, or overnight.

13 Draw the eyes on the mice and the eyelashes and brows on Little Boy Blue using the black food colouring pen.

14 Rub a little of the pink dusting powder on to Little Boy Blue's cheeks.

Twinkle, Twinkle, Little Star

Twinkle, twinkle, little star
How I wonder what you are!

You will need:

1 Victoria sponge cake (size 1)
1.925kg (4lb 5oz) fondant icing
225g (8oz) continental butter
  cream
pink, navy blue, flesh and brown
  food colouring paste
sugar glue
175g (6oz) simple pastillage
525 (1lb 2oz) modelling fondant
50g (2oz) royal icing
black food colouring pen
edible white sparkle powder

Equipment:

1 x 25 cm (10 inch) square cake
  board
2 x 25 cm (10 inch) square cake
  cards
ruler
cocktail sticks
cake smoother

small and medium heart cutters
small star cutter
medium and large blossom cutters
foam sheet
2.5 cm (1 inch) plain circle cutter
fine paintbrush
strong non-toxic tape
small shell piping nozzle
no. 2 plain piping nozzle

Colour:

Fondant icing: 450g (1lb) pink,
  1.450kg (3lb 4oz) white, 25g (1oz)
  navy blue
Pastillage: 175g (6oz) white
Modelling fondant: 150g (5oz) pale
  pink, 225g (8oz) white, 125g (4oz)
  pink, 25g (1oz) flesh
Royal icing: 25g (1oz) brown, 25g
  (1oz) white

1 Cover the cake board with 300g (11oz) of the pink fondant and put aside to dry. Using 600g (1lb 5oz) of the white fondant, roll out and cover both cake cards. Measure 5 cm (2 inches) from the top of each and mark a straight line for the picture rail.

2 Measure across each cake card, trim out lines 2.5 cm (1 inch) apart. Using 75g (3oz) of the pale pink modelling fondant, fill each line to make the wall-paper. Rub the surface to blend in the joins, using the cake smoother. With the trimmings, cut out two hearts for the wall pomander with the small heart cutter, flatten and put aside to dry.

3 Cut out the window 9 cm (3½ inches) square from the top of the picture rail. Fill with the navy blue fondant.

4 With 75g (3oz) of the white model-ling fondant, cut strips for the picture rail, window panes and cut out a sill. Roll a sausage shape for the curtain pole and a thin sausage with a nail for the wall pomander. Cut out two hearts, flatten slightly. Stick on the pomander with the two pink hearts. Make two pictures and mark the edges with a knife. Cut out the patterns, using the large heart cutter and the blossom cut-ters. Roll out and cut the star for the window, cut a tiny oblong for the pho-tograph and cut two circles for shelves, using the 2.5 cm (1 inch) circle cutter. Trim a corner in each circle and leave to dry. Put the photograph aside, then stick everything in place using a little sugar glue.

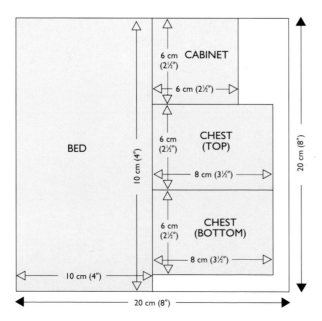

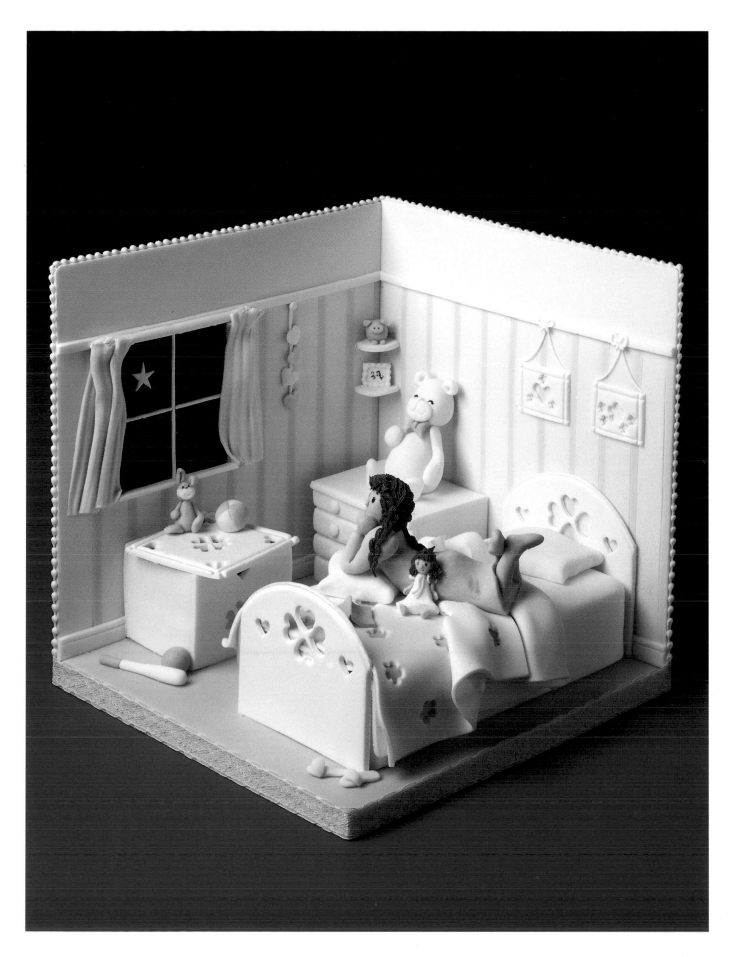

5 To make the curtains, roll out the remaining pale pink modelling fondant and cut out two 10 cm (4 inch) squares. Press the end of the paintbrush into each to pleat, then stick either side of the window.

6 Cut the cake as shown overleaf.

7 Slice a layer in the bed cake and sandwich back together, using 125g (4oz) of the continental butter cream. Using a little more butter cream, sandwich the chest of drawers together. With the remaining butter cream, spread a thin layer over the surface of each cake to help the fondant stick.

8 To make the chest of drawers, roll out and cut pieces to fit using 75g (3oz) of the white fondant. Cover the back first, then the two sides, and finally the front. Mark the lines across for the drawers, using a ruler. Cover the top, keeping an overlap at the front and round off the edge. Using the trimmings, model eight balls for the handles, stick in place with sugar glue.

9 Roll out 275g (10oz) of the white fondant and cover the bed cake completely. Model two pillows using 50g (2oz) white fondant for each, position one on the bed and put the other aside.

10 To make the toybox, roll out 125g (4oz) of the white fondant and cut pieces to fit each side with an extra 1 cm ($^1/_2$ inch) for the overlap at the top. Cut out the front, using the small heart cutter for the pattern, and position on the front of the toybox.

11 To make the toybox lid, roll out 25g (1oz) of the white pastillage and cut a square to fit. Mark the lines with a knife and cut out the pattern in the centre. Leave to dry on the foam sheet.

12 To make the headboard and footboard, split the remaining white pastillage in half, roll out and cut an 11 cm (4$^1/_2$ inch) square for the headboard and an oblong measuring 11 x 9 cm (4$^1/_2$ x 3$^1/_2$ inches) for the footboard. Trim the top of each to a curve. Cut out the pattern, using the medium and small heart cutters and leave to dry on the foam sheet.

13 Tape the cake cards on to the cake board, then tape the two cake cards together at the corner. Using 25g (1oz) of the white modelling fondant, cut a strip for the skirting board. Stick in place with a little sugar glue. Stick the headboard, pictures and two shelves in place, then position all the cakes on the cake board.

14 To make the three covers for the bed, roll out and cut two 20 cm (8 inch) squares using the remaining white fondant. With the large blossom cutter, cut out the flower design on one cover only. Using the remaining pink fondant, cut another 20 cm (8 inch) square for the blanket. 'Make' the bed with the plain white square for the sheet and with the pink blanket on top. Lay the cover with the flower design over the bed, then fold over the sheet. Position the remaining pillow on the bottom of the bed.

15 To make the little girl, model her nightdress first, using 75g (3oz) of the pink modelling fondant rolled into a sausage shape thinner at the top end. Make her two sleeves, using 15g ($^1/_2$oz) split in half and mark the pleats on each shoulder. Position her on the bed.

16 Model her head, a tiny nose, two hands and her two legs and feet using the flesh modelling fondant. Cut the top of each leg at a slant and stick everything in place using a little sugar glue. Mark her smile with a cocktail stick. Reserve the flesh modelling fondant trimmings for later.

17 With a 75g (3oz) piece of the white modelling fondant, roll a cone shape for teddy's body, make his head, mouth, nose, ears, arms and feet. Indent each ear and mark his smile. Stick him together on the chest of drawers using a little sugar glue.

18 Using the remaining flesh, pink and white modelling fondant, make the doll, the bunny, a pink piggy bank, a pink bow for teddy, a pink and white ball, two pink slippers, an open pink book for the bed, a white photograph and the pink and white bat and ball for the side of the toybox. Stick the footboard and toybox lid in place, then stick all the modelled pieces in position using a little sugar glue. Fill the heart pattern on the front of the toybox with hearts cut from a little pink modelling fondant.

19 Using the small shell nozzle and the brown royal icing, pipe the little girl's pigtails and the hair on the doll.

20 Using the white royal icing and the No. 2 piping nozzle, pipe the edge of the photograph, the picture bows and all the dots around the edge of the cake cards. Leave the cake to dry for at least 8 hours, or overnight.

21 Using the black food colouring pen, draw the eyes on the little girl, the doll, teddy and the bunny. Draw the photograph.

22 Dust a little white sparkle powder on to the window and over the bedroom scene to make it twinkle as it would do at night.

Useful Suppliers and Addresses

Blue Ribbons Cakecraft Centre
110 Walton Road
East Molesey KT8 0HP
Tel: 0181 941 1591

Blackburn's Cake Centre
108 Alexandra Drive
Surbiton KT5 9AG
Tel: 0181 399 6875

Mary Jane's Pantry
60 Church Road
Ashford
Middlesex TW15 2TS
Tel: 01784 252904

Squires Kitchen
3 Waverley Lane
Farnham
Surrey GU9 8BB
Tel: 01252 734309

Felicity Clare
360 Leach Place
Walton Summit
Bamber Bridge
Preston
Lancashire PR5 8AR
Tel: 01772 628286

A Piece of Cake
18 Upper High Street
Thame
Oxfordshire
OX9 3EX
Tel: 01844 213428

Elizabeth David Cookshop
3 North Row
The Market
Covent Garden
London
WC2 8RA
Tel: 0171 836 9167

G.T. Culpitt & Son Ltd.
Culpitt House
Place Farm
Wheathamstead
Hertfordshire
AL4 8SB
Tel: 01582 834122

British Sugarcraft Guild
Wellington House
Messeter Place
Eltham
London
SE9 5DP
Tel: 0181 859 6943

NORTH AMERICA
Maid of Scandinavia
3244 Raleigh Avenue
Minneapolis
MN 55416

Wilton Enterprises Inc
2240 West 75th Street
Woodridge
Illinois 60517

Home Cake Artistry Inc
1002 North Central
Suite 511
Richardson
Texas 75080

Creative Tools Ltd.
3 Tannery Court
Richmond Hill
Ontario
Canada L4C 7V5

AUSTRALIA
Australian National Cake
Decorators' Association
PO Box 321
Plympton SA 5038

NEW ZEALAND
New Zealand Cake Decorator's Guild
Secretary Julie Tibble
78 Kirk Street
Otaki
Wellington

SOUTH AFRICA
South African Sugarcraft Guild
National Office
1 Tuzla Mews
187 Smit Street
Fairlan 2195

Simply fill out the order form
and send it to:
Reed Book Services Ltd, PO Box 5, Rushden, Northants NN10 6YX

These books are also available from all good bookshops or by phoning through on our special CREDIT CARD HOTLINE on 01933 414000, quoting reference JS041D31C. Speak to our customer service team during office hours (9am to 5pm) or leave a message on the answer machine, quoting your full credit card number, plus expiry date, and your full name and address.

Offers available to UK only. While every effort is made to keep the prices low, the publisher reserves the right to increase prices at short notice.

Your order will be dispatched within 28 days, subject to availability. You may photocopy this order form.

Registered office Michelin House, 81 Fulham Road, London SW3 6RB. Registered in England No 1974080

JS041D31C

OTHER TITLES AVAILABLE	PRICE	QUANTITY	TOTAL
Debbie Brown's Party Cakes	£5.99		£
Debbie Brown's Saucy Cakes	£5.99		£
		POSTAGE & PACKING £	1.00
		GRAND TOTAL £	

NAME

ADDRESS

POSTCODE

I ENCLOSE A CHEQUE/POSTAL ORDER £   made payable to **Reed Book Services Ltd**

OR PLEASE DEBIT MY ACCESS ☐ VISA ☐ AMEX ☐ DINERS CARD ☐

NUMBER ☐☐☐☐ ☐☐☐☐ ☐☐☐☐ ☐☐☐

BY £   EXPIRY DATE ☐☐☐☐ SIGNATURE

☐ If you do not wish your details to be used for promotional purposes by Reed International Books. or other carefully selected companies, please tick this box.

$\mathcal{I}ndex$

·············

A
apricot glaze 16

B
baking tins, lining 22
blossom cutters 20, 22
brushes 20
butter cream 17

C, D
cake boards 18, 22
cake recipes 6-12
chocolate butter cream 17
Cinderella 60-3
cocktail sticks 20
colouring 20, 21, 22
continental butter cream 17
craft knives 20
crimping tools 20, 22
cutters 20
dowelling 20

E
Elves and the Shoemaker 34-6
embossing stamps 20
equipment 18-20

F
fillings 16-17
flowers, blossom 20, 22

foam 20
fondant icing 14
  colouring 21
  covering cake
  boards 22
  modelling 14-15
  rolling out 21
  sticking together 22
frill cutters 20, 22
fruit cake, rich 12

G
garrett frill cutters 20, 22
glaze, apricot 16
glue 15, 20
Goldilocks and the Three
  Bears 64-6
greaseproof paper piping
bags 18, 23
gum arabic 20

H, I
Hansel and Gretel 40-3
icings 14-15
  colouring 21

J, K
Jack and the Beanstalk 27-9
Jack and Jill 76-8
knives 20

L
lemon curd 16
Little Boy Blue 82-3

Little Jack Horner 70-2
Little Miss Muffet 79-81
Little Red Riding Hood 54-6

M, N
Madeira cake 6-7
marble cake, pink 10
marzipan 16
modelling fondant 14-15
modelling tools 20
nozzles, piping 18

P
paintbrushes 20
pastillage, simple 15
pens, food colouring 20
pink marble cake 10
pins 20
piping bags 18, 23
piping nozzles 18
powder colours 20, 22
Princess and the Pea 47-9
Puss-in-Boots 37-9

Q, R
quick mix cake 8-9
Rapunzel 24-6
ribbons 20
rolling pins 18
royal icing 15, 21
rulers 20
Rumpelstiltskin 57-9

S
skewers 20
smoothers 20, 22
Snow White and
  the Seven Dwarfs 30-3
sponge cakes 8-9
sugar glue 15

T
Three Little Pigs 50-3
Thumbelina 44-6
turntables 18-20
Twinkle, Twinkle, Little
  Star 84-6
Two Little Dicky Birds
  73-5

U, V
Ugly Duckling 67-9
Victoria sponge
  cake 8